Happiness in Totality

BY ANVI DARDA

© Anvi Darda 2021
All rights reserved
All rights reserved by author. No part of this publication may be reproduced, stored in a retrieval system or transmitted in any form or by any means, electronic, mechanical, photocopying, recording or otherwise, without the prior permission of the author.
Although every precaution has been taken to verify the accuracy of the information contained herein, the author and publisher assume no responsibility for any errors or omissions. No liability is assumed for damages that may result from the use of information contained within.
First Published in August 2021

ISBN: 978-93-5472-340-7

BLUEROSE PUBLISHERS
www.bluerosepublishers.com
info@bluerosepublishers.com
+91 8882 898 898
Cover Design:
Muskaan Sachdeva
Typographic Design:
Ilma Mirza
Distributed by: BlueRose, Amazon, Flipkart

Dedication

I would like to dedicate this book to my parents: Abhay Darda and Varsha Darda, who always supported me and pushed me to achieve my absolute best.

MY BIO

Anvi Abhay Darda is 21 years old and finished her schooling from Delhi Public School, Pune. She did her graduation in BBA-IB from MITSOM College, Pune. She is currently doing masters in commerce from BMCC, Pune along with diploma in marketing and business administration from Symbiosis school of business, Pune. Her hobbies include reading and dancing. Along with this she is also a national gold medallist in archery. She has done various courses in physiology, photography, makeup and hair, baking and bag designing. Her love for reading is what pushed her towards dreaming of becoming an author since she was a kid. Her aim or goal in life is to help others and make their life better even if in a small way.

INDEX

INTRODUCTION

"There is no path to happiness: happiness is the path."

Buddha

"Happiness is when what you think, what you say and what you do are in harmony."

Mahatma Gandhi

"There is no key to happiness; the door is always open."

Mother Teresa

In all religions, cultures and eras, people have always talked about the importance of finding peace of mind and living a happy life. As humans evolved, their need to live a happy life grew with it too. Right from the fifteenth century to the twenty-first century, all great leaders have talked about following a path of greatness and fulfilment, which ultimately leads us to a lifetime of happiness. There are two basic things which drive every human, no matter what colour, gender or age they are. First, is our will to survive no matter what life throws at us; second, is to be happy regardless of what happens to us. Can we think of anyone who does not naturally crave these two outcomes? In the absence of these two things, our life would have no meaning.

It is essential to find true happiness in order to give meaning to our life. Happiness is about living a life of contentment and satisfaction where we may not have everything we need, but we stay eternally grateful for all we have. Happiness is about finding the best in everything and looking at life with a positive perspective. Bad things happen to everyone as a consequence, but a happy person knows how to gain the most from it and come out of it with a smile on their face. A happy person is not someone who smiles a lot, but it is someone who does not need anyone to make him happy. When a person finds happiness within themselves and knows how to stay happy, regardless of the changes in the external environment, that is when the person finds true happiness.

True happiness is always inside ourselves. It is about enjoying our own company and living in harmony with our body, mind and soul. It refers to being in love with ourselves, always. A person who can love themself freely is always someone who is closer to living a lifetime of happiness. Happiness is ultimately the love of life and the celebration of the living. It is not a by-product of a situation or circumstance that happens to our liking. It is rather a choice; choosing to be happy, bringing us closer to our self and pushing us in the right direction in life. Living a happy life helps us enjoy everything around us. It makes us appreciate and love the beautiful life that we are gifted with.

Everything around us brings with it a reason to be happy. All we need to do is see it with love in our eyes and kindness in our heart. The places of happiness are infinite and its sources are never-ending. We derive happiness from those places because we have opened our hearts and allowed them in. Everyone finds happiness differently, but none of us always stay happy. We let so many things come between us and our happiness, when all we really need to do is find it inside ourselves. A happy person is not someone who does not feel sad, but is someone who can overcome that sadness or pain and move towards greater things in life.

LACK OF HAPPINESS

What happens when there is no happiness in our life?

1. War and terrorism

War and terrorism always starts when there is hatred filled in the hearts of people or when they are constantly made to believe in something bad. Our mind is like a baby's. It is innocent; what we feed it with is what stays there. So, if we constantly think negatively and let our negative emotions grow, we are more likely to act that way because that is what stays most on our minds. This is why it is extremely important for us to think and feel good things, and for our minds to be positively-driven. If we are happy and content with our life, we are less likely to do something like this. This is why it is so important for us to stay happy.

2. Depression

People who are not happy or content with their life are naturally unhappy with it. When we are unhappy with our life, we pull towards our self a lot of negative emotions – one of which is depression. If something bad or wrong happens to us and we are sad as a result of it, that is not depression – that is sadness. Sadness is momentary, while depression stays longer. Depression is when we continuously feel bad every day we wake up.

We don't feel like getting out of bed, going out and meeting people, and no matter what we do, we always feel unhappy. We might smile but we are dying within us. Depression consumes our mind, body and soul and pulls us back from feeling anything good.

3. Anger

Anger is an emotion which is there in each and every one of us, regardless of the fact whether we are a child or a 70-year-old adult. Our need to react to everything that happens to us is the root cause of our anger. Anger comes from a lot of places like our ego, sensitivity, dissatisfaction from our life, and so on. We get angry when something does not go our way or when someone says something we don't like. We instantly get hyper and get angry at that person. However, being angry a lot takes a toll on our health and mental state. It pushes us to be very unhappy, and say and do very unpleasant things. Every emotion is good, to a limit. Being angry a lot affects each and every part of our life.

4. Meaningless life

Whatever we do in life or try to achieve is only for our self and our family. We try to find happiness in the little things we do to make them smile. However, if everyone around us is happy when we achieve something but *we* are not, then we feel lost and empty from within. Our achievements, no matter how big or small, mean nothing to us. Living a life where we are unhappy only makes us feel more demotivated and brings more misery along with it. We stop enjoying our work and everything we do. If we live like this every day, we are more likely to go into depression. Living a life without happiness always feels meaningless and depressing. What is the whole point of living like that?

5. Mental illness

Mental illness could be called an extreme, long-term depression. Mental illness takes a toll on our mind, body and behaviour. It leads to a persistently depressed mood, loss of interest in doing anything, and crying out-of-the-blue when we do not even know what is wrong with us or why we are even crying. A person who has everything in life, like money, fame, popularity, could also suffer from mental illnesses. It is difficult to know the root cause of mental illness, but it is a disorder which makes it very difficult for people to survive and hence, many commit suicide. Therefore, when we start seeing signs of mental illness in ourselves or people around us, it is best to speak to a therapist or consult a psychologist.

6. Careless

A person who is unhappy in their own life and just living each day as it goes no longer has goals or dreams in life, or anything that could excite him or make him happy. A person who, in the most basic sense, is simply surviving, not living their life or feeling alive, would hardly care about anyone else. A person who is just living his life as a routine would never go out of his way to make anyone else happy, because he is not happy with his life itself. Such a person would never indulge in social work or do something good for the society because of his attitude towards life as a whole. A person like this will spend their entire life complaining and making others miserable, instead of being happy and making others happy.

7. Fear

All of us have fears within us. While some of us are scared of darkness, snakes, ghosts, etc., others might be scared of different things. Everyone has different fears, but the fact that we are all scared of something bonds all of us. Our fears might be the result of a mind block or something deeper within us. However, our fears have a way of taking control over our body and mind. It is a known fact that a person who is unhappy in life has more fears than someone who is happy. Happy people have the strength to face and overcome their fears. Unhappy people, on the other hand, develop more fears and live with them. This affects their relationships, work and other areas of life, as these fears keep pulling them back.

8. Anxiety

We all worry, get anxious or scared at some points in our life. But we don't dwell on those feelings. It is caused by a particular situation and when that situation gets resolved, those feelings go away with it. However, not everyone feels anxious that rarely. Some people face it in their day-to-day life. Such people constantly worry, fear and feel anxious about everything. They overthink every situation a lot and, due to this, its impact can be seen on their body, mind and behaviour. Anxiety is a disorder which can also cause panic attacks. It also leads to extreme restlessness and it can drive a person crazy. It is best to contact a psychologist to treat an anxiety disorder.

9. Hatred

Love and hate are two very powerful emotions. While love makes everything worthwhile and keeps us happy, hating something has the exact opposite effect on us. When we hate something, we have so many negative emotions stored for that thing or person that when someone we hate comes in front of us, our entire day can go bad. Hatred removes the joy and happiness from everything. It fills our mind with so many negative emotions that we stop seeing the good in anything; we stop enjoying things, and we start complaining and being grumpy about everything. People who are very unhappy in life start hating their life and everything associated with it, and they fall in a vicious circle of darkness.

10. Pain

We all go through pain at some point in our life. We all feel betrayal, heartbreak and loss. However, a person who is living a happy life will come out of it much easily in comparison to someone who is unhappy. This is because of the fact that when someone is happy, they also start being more positive and motivated; they discover themselves and their strength, and they tend to have a good support system to pull them out of it. Such people face their pain with courage, learn something out of it and move on in life. While a person who is unhappy will find another reason to add to their misery, and will continue to drown in their pain and be more unhappy.

11. Boredom

We are all living in a fast-moving world where everyone is busy with their lives. People have work or something or the other planned out for the day. We always like utilising our free time so that we don't get bored. But when we are sitting at home with nothing new to do, no plans, or when everyone around us is busy, we tend to get very bored. Boredom is when we don't enjoy something we do. When this happens for a lot of days, boredom strikes us, as has happened in the lockdown initiated due to the coronavirus. When we are not happy doing something, we naturally get bored doing it. This is why it is important for us to do things which make us happy and also find happiness in everything so that we can enjoy it.

12. Dissatisfaction

Unhappiness and dissatisfaction are majorly linked. Whenever we are unhappy doing something, we also feel dissatisfied doing it, and whenever we do not feel satisfied doing something, we do not feel like doing that anymore. This is because when something does not bring us satisfaction, we do not enjoy doing it. As a result, we feel more detached from that thing. Similarly, when we feel dissatisfied with our life, we also start being more unhappy with it. A person who is extremely unhappy with their life is more likely to be depressed and start being unhappy about everything associated with their life and, as a result, they are more likely to attract bad things their way.

13. Worry

We are all worried about something or the other. While some of us worry about marks, some worry about work, some worry about having a good life, while some worry about something as basic as what-to-wear, and the list goes on. We worry about the basic things to the most complex things in life. However, when we worry too much, we start overthinking, stressing and being tense. The funny thing is that the more we think, the more we worry, and the more we stress. So, it is all inter-related. However, people who are unhappy worry more than people who are happy, as they are also very sensitive. So they tend to worry more about everything. This leads them to take more stress, which also spoils their health.

14. Self-hate

In today's world, it is extremely important for us to love our self, because at the end of day we are all we've got. It is extremely important for us to indulge in self-care and pampering, so that we can keep loving our self. But, loving our self is never easy because as much as we know our strengths, we also know our weakness; as much as we know the good things we have done, we also know the bad things we have done, and we don't forgive our self for those things. So, self-love is difficult for us. Especially for someone who is unhappy with themselves and their life, they hate themselves even more. It doesn't matter how much the people around them say good, because internally they are still hurting.

15. Suicides

The whole reason why someone does something as extreme as killing themselves is because they are extremely unhappy with their life. Every day is a struggle for such people. Their will to die becomes much more than their will to live. For most of us, one reason is enough for us to survive to keep going. But people who commit suicide have either lost that reason along with their will to live, or they are surrounded by so much darkness that they cannot see that reason. In India, someone commits suicide every 4 minutes. It is extremely sad and disheartening. If only everyone could find their way to happiness, hold on, stay strong and fight their demons, will this world be a better place to live.

QUESTIONS

1. What makes you instantly happy?
2. Do you really know what makes you unhappy? If yes, what are you doing to deal with it?
3. On a scale of 1 to 10, how happy are you in your life?
4. If, in the previous question, your answer was not a perfect 10, how do you plan to get there?
5. What is more important according to you: loving yourself or loving others? Are you sure it should not be the other way round?
6. If we know how important it is to be happy, why are we not working on it all the time?
7. Does most of the misery in our life come from the situation around us or how we deal with it?
8. Are you really willing to do what it takes to live a life of abundant peace and happiness?

IMPORTANCE OF HAPPINESS

1. It makes us healthier

People who are happy in life are less likely to fall sick because they keep working on their body, mind and soul. Also, if a happy person falls sick or gets a disease, it is much easier for them to recover from that than others, as a happy mind is a positive mind. The more we stay positive and think positive thoughts about our recovery, the more we attract that towards ourselves and that is more likely to happen. Also, it is a known fact that happy people recover at a much faster rate than others. This is because such people do not pay much attention to their pain; they still know how to look at the bright side of life and smile their way through everything. This gives hope not only to them, but also to their family and their doctor.

2. It leads us to becoming more financially successful

Being happy has a huge impact on our success. People who are happy are more motivated and driven in life. They are also people who have high dreams and goals and work hard to fulfil them. People who are unhappy with their jobs, business or lives are unlikely to find and utilise new opportunities in their respective fields. A person who is happy is also someone who is full of energy and life. This encourages other workers to be the same way. Every business has its ups and downs; a person who is positive and happy in life is more likely to recover from this and move on. But, most importantly, a happy person – instead of complaining – always feels grateful about everything he has, and this positivity helps him attract more in life.

3. It helps in loving our self

It is extremely important for us to love our self and appreciate our self. This not only helps us to know our value and how much we deserve, but also to respect our self and take a stand for our self when needed. People who are happy with their lives are more likely to love themselves than those who don't, because true happiness always comes from loving our self and finding meaning in life. People who are unhappy with things around them also tend to be unhappy with themselves. Such people find it extremely difficult to love themselves or their life, because they do not see anything good in it. At the end of the day, we can only give what we have. So, if we cannot truly love ourselves, we cannot even love anyone else.

4. It helps in maintaining balance in work and personal life

In life, it is crucial to maintain a balance between our work, friends and personal life. Until this balance is maintained, we flourish in each part of our life. But the moment this balance breaks, problems start arising. Hence, the secret to a happy life is maintaining the balance between our work and personal life, no matter how hard things get. Otherwise, we will end up being a workaholic, with no time left for our family. This will not only make them unhappy, but it will make us feel bad because there will be so many important moments in life that we will miss out on. Our family is the most important thing to us, but we sometimes forget that while running behind our goals. A happy person is someone who maintains this balance and moves ahead in life.

5. It leads to people surrounding us feeling more happy

When we step out in the real world, we meet so many people. However, we enjoy the company of those who are always happy and full of life, in comparison to those who are dull and boring. This is because such people are more fun to be around, are full of exciting ideas and have high hopes for their future. That is why it is so important for us to be so happy. By being happy with ourselves and our lives, we feel good, but we also help everyone around us feel the same way. We also become someone whom everyone loves being around. By being happy, we inspire others to be the same way and motivate them to deal with all of their problems with a smile on their face. A happy person is someone who can help others be the same way.

6. It gives meaning to our life

When we become really old, and we are living our last few moments, we all want to look back at a life where we are happy and satisfied. We all want to live a life where we lived to our fullest, did crazy things together, overcame our fears and did things that challenged us. We run behind money all our life but, in the end, we all wish for a life of fulfilment. Happiness helps us in living a life like that. It pushes us to do things which make us feel alive like adventure activities, learning new things, and so on. A happy person is more likely to live a life that is good, meaningful and worthwhile than someone who is unhappy. Happiness gives meaning to our life and everything we do. As a result, a happy person ends up living a life that he will not look back at and regret, but smile at instead.

7. It helps us in achieving our goals in life

Happy people are more likely to achieve their goals in life because they are full of energy and, hence, feel more motivated to do things. They are full of positivity and always want to learn new things. Also, happy people set smarter, attainable goals, which pushes them to work hard towards them. Such people also have high willpower and are more determined to achieve all their goals in life. A happy mind is also more likely to come up with more creative ideas, as it is full of energy and good things. Our mindset plays a huge role in how we see things in life. A person with a positive and happy mindset takes every difficulty as a challenge and does not give up easily in life. It is these qualities or traits in them which help living a life that most people only dream of.

8. It makes us more generous

It is our moral responsibility to help those less privileged than us. We can do this with the help of social work and donations to the needy. This will not only make their lives better but, with their love and good wishes, it also helps to make our life better. Life is not about what we get, but it is truly about how much we give, because the more we give, the more comes back to us through karma. People who are happy and content in their life engage more in social work than people who are unhappy. This is because happy people are more generous and giving. They like making others smile and making a difference in their lives. This is exactly why happy people grow more, because they also give more.

9. It helps in dealing with stress, pain and trauma

We all go through so much pain, stress and trauma in our day-to-day lives. The scars such incidents put on us stay for life. However, people who are happy deal with their problems in a much better way than people who are not. This is because such people know how to look at the bright side of life, face challenges with courage and overcome them. Happy people also know how to deal with their emotions in a much better and calmer manner. This also makes them stronger than others. Everyone faces problems and trauma in life. No one is immune to it and no one can run from it. The only difference between people who stay happy, as compared to people who are not, is how they face their problems. That is what makes all the difference in the world.

10. It helps us in finding our purpose in life

We are all born on this earth with a specific purpose in our lives. While some spend a lifetime finding this purpose, some already know it. When we start living a happy life, we move closer to finding our purpose and living a life filled with goodness. Without happiness, our life has no meaning. Achieving true happiness is one of the most important purposes of our life. Happiness does not only make us appreciate everything we have, but it also makes us value it. It helps us make the bad things good, and the good things better. It teaches us the true meaning of our lives. People who live an unhappy life never find the true meaning or purpose of it, and end up missing out on so much.

11. It helps in maintaining good relations

We are social beings and we are dependent on others for love, happiness and care. We expect others to give us all those things which we cannot give ourselves. This is why it is important for us to have a social life and people we can count on in our life. However, due to time, distance and our busy lives, maintaining good relations with people is never easy. Most people who are unhappy in life do not even try to stay in touch, because they have so many problems of their own that they do not give their friends the time they deserve. Happy people, on the other hand, are more effective in making long-lasting relations. They also know how to prioritize important things in life and are much better in maintaining good relations with people.

12. It helps us sleep more peacefully

It is very important for us to sleep eight hours in a day. This helps our brain, eyes and our mind to get the rest it needs to function properly. People who sleep late tend to be more tired the next day. This effect can be seen on their face as they look more tired and start getting dark circles below their eyes. While some people still sleep late due to a bad habit, many people have sleeping problems. They have so much tension and stress, which keeps them awake at night and does not let them get a peaceful night's sleep. Even when such people sleep, their mind does not fully relax. People who are happy with their day, sleep more peacefully than those who aren't. Such people feel fresh after they get up, are more prone to get good dreams, and also have a great day ahead.

13. It helps us stay calmer and more composed

The biggest weakness some of us have is anger and giving a reaction to every negative thing that life throws at us. Even when we want to, we do not know how to deal with every situation with elegance and grace. We let other people affect us, spoil our mood and we end up doing unpleasant things as a result of it, which we always regret later. One very effective way of staying calm and more composed is by practicing meditation. Meditation helps us to stay happy and see the best in every situation that is presented to us. It calms us down and helps us to think things through before giving a reaction to anything. Unhappy people tend to react more because of their sensitivity, while happy people know to deal with things by staying calm and maintaining their decorum.

14. It helps us increase life expectancy

We all want to live as long as we can. We want to have kids, watch them be successful in life, get them married and then watch our grandkids grow. At every stage of our life, we have so much to look forward to; we have so many moments to live, and so many moments to watch. However, not everyone can live until all this happens. Death is inevitable but there is one way by which we can live longer – that is by being happy. Happy people are less likely to suffer from illnesses or diseases because they are more proactive in life. Even if they do fall sick, they recover at a much faster rate, as compared to unhappy people, because happy people are positively-driven. They do not give up. They keep pushing their mind to fight any illness and survive. Their will to live is also more, which helps them stay alive.

15. It helps promote peace in the world

All those people who engage in violent activities, like terrorism or bombings, are more inclined to do something like this due to extreme unhappiness with their lives. This is also why they don't care how many lives they destroy, because they only want to spread pain. But a happy person always wants to spread smiles and make everyone happy around him. This is why when we are happy with our life and surroundings, we would never engage in something like this. We can think more clearly about what we are doing and its impact on people. Happy people are also more loving and compassionate. They love more, they smile more and help people deal with their negativity. Hence, even if in a small way, we are promoting peace in this world by just being happy and making this world a much better place to live in.

16. It ensures we live a life we never regret

When we look back at our life, we regret those times we wasted being unhappy and angry, or those times where we didn't live to our fullest. Our school or college times are when we wish we had more fun, but we cannot do anything about it now. If we are still living a dull, boring life, we will probably look back and regret this too. It is so important for us to make the most out of every moment we live in order to live a life without regrets. Living a happy life helps us to do this. It helps us to make the most of every moment we are present in by living it to the fullest. A happy person feels alive at every moment. Hence, they are more likely to live a happy life which they will never regret, while an unhappy person will continue leading an unhappy life which he will look back at and regret.

17. It brings us closer to spirituality

Whenever we have a lot of pain or problems in life, we always go to a temple to worship God. At the end of the day, whether we believe in God or not, God is the only saviour who solves all our problems. Due to this, we have undying faith and believe in God. This faith helps us get through anything in life. We all wish to be connected to God. Meditation helps us to stay connected with the supreme power above and brings us closer to spirituality. Being closer to our spiritual self helps us stay strong in times of need and gives meaning to our life. Spiritual people have positive relations, are more optimistic and follow a strong purpose in life. Happy people are known to be more spiritual than those who are unhappy with their lives.

QUESTIONS

1. Is it important to be successful in order to be happy? If yes, can't a poor man be happy?
2. In life, what is more important: to have everything we want or to be happy with everything we get?
3. If happiness and sadness are two parts of a coin, can we not choose to be happy, regardless of what situation life throws at us?
4. We are always postponing our happiness for the next big thing we achieve but even when we get that, are we really happy?
5. We look for happiness in the outside world when it is within our self. Are we looking for happiness in all the wrong places?
6. Whose responsibility is it to make us happy: our family, friends or our self?
7. Is money a good indicator for our happiness? Does having more money really bring more happiness with it?
8. Is being too happy a bad thing?

MYTHS OF HAPPINESS

1. Being successful brings happiness

Most people think that they need to be successful in order to be happy. But no one is successful at all times in their life. Life comes with its ups and downs. If we can be happy when everything is going well, we should also know how to be happy when things are not going well. Happiness is not only about making the most out of the good moments, but also about making the most out of the inevitable bad ones. Everyone can be happy when things are going well, but only a truly happy and strong person can smile even when things are bad.

2. People who smile a lot are crazy

If we see someone smiling alone for no reason or in their toughest times, when they should be crying, we think they must be crazy or something is wrong with them. However, such people are not crazy – they are just happy all the time. People who are happy by themselves don't need anyone else to please them. They can smile on their own, even in tough situations. This does not make them crazy, but it shows that they value their happiness. There is nothing wrong with being happy or smiling. So, stay happy, always.

3. Happiness is not long-lasting

Most of us believe that happiness is not long-lasting. When someone does something for us, we feel good and happy but that feeling passes away with that moment and we are no longer happy. When we depend on the external environment for our happiness, then our happiness is more likely to be momentary because external things and situations don't always work in our favour. But when we feel happy from within and become the source of our own happiness, then we have the power to be happy, always.

4. Being happy is a privilege

Poor people or middle-class people think that being happy is a privilege that only the rich have because they have everything. They have a big house, cars, a successful business and everything they wished for. Such people keep using their situation as an excuse to be unhappy. However, rich people are under so much tension and stress because of their business and social pressure that they are unhappy too. So this raises the question: who really is happy in life? Or, does everyone just have excuses for their unhappiness?

5. Loving others will make us happier and our life better

While we believe that the more love we give, the more love we always get back, however, we can only give to others what we have. So, if we don't love our self, we probably can't love anyone else fully. Also, we would feel really lost in life if we keep giving others all the love we should give our self. Loving others does not make our life happier or better. Even if we derive happiness from that, it will hurt a lot when the other person does not value it or does not reciprocate those efforts. So, if we really want to be happy, we should start by loving our self first.

6. Special things have to happen to us for us to be happy

Almost everyone believes that we need a reason to be happy. Special things have to happen to us in order for us to be happy, like someone should buy us a gift, take us on a trip , throw us a party, and so on. While we are all happy in those moments, that happiness goes as quickly as it comes. This will keep happening if we depend on the external environment for our happiness. In order to always be happy, do special things and pamper yourself. Go on a date with yourself, do things you love, celebrate yourself, because this is the only thing which we have control over.

7. People are unhappy due to their circumstances or situations in life

We believe that when someone is very sad or unhappy, it is because of the situation or circumstances they are going through, or went through, in life. However, this is not at all true. When someone is unhappy in life, it is not because of what they are going through but because of their inability to deal with that thing effectively and come out of it. Such people keep using their bad phase as an excuse to stay unhappy. At the end of the day, everyone goes through bad times. It is how we deal with it that makes all the difference in the world.

8. No one is truly happy in life

People who are unhappy in life keep finding more reasons to stay that way. One thing they keep believing is that no one is truly happy in life. This makes them feel better in order to stay sad or unhappy. Regardless of this, our lives and our happiness are our responsibilities. If someone else chooses to live an unhappy life, it is not necessary for us to make the same choice. We can rise above that and choose to be happy. This will not only make our life better, but also of the people who are around us.

9. People who are too happy are either on drugs or into something bad

When we see someone around us who is full of life and energy and is always pumped up, even on early Monday mornings, we naturally think that this person is on drugs or into something bad. It is not normal for us to see someone so happy and excited about everything. We would rather be surrounded by people who hate their lives and keep complaining about it. But, is it really necessary for us to turn something as good as someone being truly happy into some negative assumptions about what that person might be into? Why can't we be completely happy or let others be that way?

10. It makes people selfish

Many people think that being happy would make them selfish, as they would only start thinking about their happiness. They then would not do much to make others happy. However, it is a known fact that happy people are much more generous than unhappy people. People who love themselves and are happy with their lives make everyone around them happy. They love more, give more and care more. If we are happy in our life, only then can we make others happy in theirs; it all starts with us. So, be happy with yourself. There is absolutely nothing selfish about it.

11. Having a bad past will never lead us to a good future

Most of us are haunted by our past, which ruins our present and keeps spoiling our future. Everyone has a past, but the people who overcome it are the people who decided to move on, make the most of their present and move towards a happy future. When we go through something bad, it is up to us if we want to learn from it and move ahead in life, or keep holding onto it and let it pull us back. So, it is not necessary that people with a bad past do not have a good future. That totally depends on us, and whether we let our past go or not. If we let go of our past, then there are infinite possibilities for our future. But if we keep holding onto it, it will limit us, always.

12. More money equals to more happiness

We run our entire life behind money. When we finally have more money, we run behind materialistic things, thinking that the more we buy, the happier we will be. However, money can only buy us a good lifestyle, not a happy life. We all make the mistake of associating money with happiness, but they are not related. Even someone living on the street with absolutely nothing can be happier than someone living in a big, posh bungalow. Money can buy a lot of things but a happy and good life cannot be bought – it is to be found and lived. Money was never an indication for happiness. More money never means more happiness. More satisfaction and acceptance in life leads to more happiness.

PROCESS OF HAPPINESS

1. Stay calm

Whenever something upsets us or makes us angry, it is always best to stay calm. We can do this by taking deep breaths in and out, until we calm down. This will help us think more practically, and not say or do something which we might regret later. Staying calm helps us to deal with the situation in a much better manner and it helps us to think things through.

For example – if we are stuck in traffic, getting angry or frustrated is not going to help us reach anywhere faster. It will take as much time as it has to, regardless of how we react. So, choose to be calm in that situation.

2. Understanding the problem

If something is bothering us, it is always good to understand the root cause of the problem. We need to understand what, exactly, the problem is and why it is happening. When we know the problem and how we feel about it, it becomes much easier to accept it and understand the other person's point of view.

For example - if someone is talking bad about us behind our back and that is making us upset: now we know the root cause and how we feel about it, so it is much easier for us to deal with it.

3. Think from the other person's point of view

Most of our problems arise from the fact that we don't understand the other person's perspective or motive behind it. So, try putting yourself in their shoes and try understanding why they did what they did, or what pushed to do something like that. Sometimes, their method might be wrong but their intentions behind doing that might be good. So, even if we can forgive them after understanding their point of view, it is best to let go, and if we still can't we, should move to the next step.

For example - when our parents shout at us, we might feel bad. But, their intentions behind that are good. When we realise that, it is easier to understand them.

4. Communicate

Communication is the key to problem-solving. Sometimes we misunderstand the other person or make our own assumptions. This makes us think or believe things which are not even true. So, it is always best if we communicate with the person with whom we have a problem. A lot of times, the problem gets solved just by communicating, as the other person realises their mistake and they can find a solution together.

For example – if there is a misunderstanding between us and our friend, simply communicating and talking about it will solve the problem.

5. Forgive them

After communicating with the other person, if that person realizes their mistake or if the misunderstanding gets sorted out, it is best to forgive them and whatever happened because holding onto it is going to do us no good. It will only add more problems in our life. If the other person does not realize their mistakes even after we tell them, then just let them be; that shows their understanding level. Be the greater person, forgive that person and free yourself from that problem. Let karma deal with such people.

For example – if your brother hurts you by saying something really awful and you tell him how you feel about it and how much that hurts you, but he still does not realize his mistake, then be the greater person and let it go. He will understand as he grows.

6. Can you solve your problem?

If, after communicating, the problem is still there in our mind, then we need to ask our self: can we do anything about the problem or solve it? If the answer is yes, then do what needs to be done to make it go away. If not, then there is no point holding onto it as this will only cause us more pain. We need to understand, then, that we need to let go and stop crying about it.

For example – if someone's death is making us very upset, it is okay to mourn, be angry or miss that person. But, by doing all this, will that person come back? No.

We need to understand this and, after a point of time, continue with our regular life.

7. Grateful

Always feel grateful for everything life throws at you, be it a problem or opportunity. Any problem we face, even if it's really bad, is still not as worse as it could be. So we still have something to be grateful for. God is still saving us from the worst. Everything that happens in our life, happens for good – we may not realise it now, but someday we will. So keep reminding yourself of that. It helps us get through things positively, and attract greatness our way. If something does not work out right now, it's only because we deserve better.

For example – if we really wanted to make a deal with some foreign company but it does not go through, we will be obviously upset because of it. But, due to this, we could sign a deal with a much bigger company in a year or two. We don't know what life has in store for us. So just trust it. Whatever happens is always for the best.

8. Learn from our mistakes

After being grateful and seeing the good in the bad things that happen to us, it is important for us to learn from our mistakes. As much as we think we are always right, that is never the case. Mistakes always happen from both ends. Even if we are not at fault, we let that thing happen to us. Right there is our mistake. So it is very important for us to identify our mistakes, so that we can learn from them and move on.

For example – if we learn something for the first time, we are bound to make mistakes. But if we keep learning from those mistakes as we move forward, we will keep growing in life.

9. Make sure those mistakes are not repeated

It is not only important for us to learn, but also for us to implement our learnings in our life and make sure that those mistakes are not repeated again. Making mistakes is okay, but making the same mistakes again is stupidity. Then we stay stuck in life and the same things keep happening to us again and again. This is why learning from our mistakes is so important. This helps us avoid the same things happening to us and helps us live a much better life.

For example – if we make cake for the first time, we might make mistakes. But when we understand where we went wrong and learn from it, we are likely to make a better cake next time.

10. Move on

For you to move on, all you need to do is find your way to happiness and everything else will be okay. Moving on takes time and it is difficult, but, with time, all your wounds will be healed. Just deal with it one day at a time and start doing more of those things which make you happy, like going out with your friends, shopping or whatever else. Instead of sitting at home, crying and focusing on your wounds, try doing something that drives you crazy, like some adventure activity. The happier you are, the easier it is to move on. The more you sit at home and cry, the more pain grows because you're focusing so much on it. It may take time, but you will move on. Stay happy, stay positive.

For example – if someone breaks your heart, instead of crying about it every day, gather yourself together and do things which make you happy. Our life is about what we attract. So instead of attracting pain, attract happiness towards yourself.

11. Love yourself

Moving on from one bad situation is not enough because life will keep throwing more bad things at us. In order to deal with all of them effectively, it is extremely important for us to love our self. When we love our self, we stay away from things or situations that do not deserve us and we attract more good things our way. When we start loving our self, our happiness becomes our topmost priority and we are likely to live a happy life.

For example – When you start loving yourself, you will naturally stop running behind people who don't value you and start being around people who truly appreciate you and love you for who you are.

IMPACT OF HAPPINESS

1. It makes us more compassionate

Happy people are more loving and caring. They love making others happy. As a result, they are also more compassionate in life as compared to others.

2. It makes us more creative and smarter

The brain of a happy mind works more than others, as they are always fresh and full of energy, this makes them think more creatively and make smarter decisions.

3. It helps us to inspire other people

By living a happy life, a happy person inspires others to be the same way and to deal with their problems with a smile on their face.

4. It makes us more positive

Happy people know how to see the best in everything. They also know how to deal with bad times effectively. This helps them in thinking and being more positive.

5. It makes us more motivated

Happy people are more likely to find happiness in everything they do. They also love to learn more. This helps them stay motivated and give their best.

6. It makes us more energetic and fun to be around

People who are happy all the time are full of life and positivity. They are always excited to do things. This makes them more fun to be around.

7. It helps us to be our true selves

Happy people accept themselves the way they are, with their flaws and imperfections. That is why it is easier for them to be themselves all the time.

8. It helps us make better decisions

Happy people are able to think calmly, in a more composed manner, and see the bigger picture. This helps them in making better decisions.

9. It makes us value our happiness

Once we know that we deserve every bit of happiness life brings us, we start staying away from things and situations that make us unhappy because we start valuing our happiness.

10. It makes us strong

Happy people face their problems with courage and strength. They also accept their problems and move on easily. This makes them strong and helps them grow in life.

11. It makes us more productive at work

Happy people are very focused, goal-oriented and ambitious in life. They love challenges and they know their aim in life, which helps them be more productive.

12. It protects our heart

Happy people start having strong instincts due to their positive aura. This saves them from making bad decisions and protects them from heartbreak most of the time.

13. It makes us respect our life more

Once we know that we are meant to live a good and happy life we stop settling for a mediocre life and we start respecting and valuing our life more.

14. It helps in loving our self

A happy person finds it easier to love themselves by forgiving themselves for their mistakes and not being too harsh on themselves. They simply accept themselves for who they are.

15. It helps us in living a life of abundance and greatness

Happy people are also people who are very positive in life. This positivity helps in attracting more good things and living a life of abundance and greatness.

QUESTIONS

1. When you are old, weak and living your last few days, what kind of life do you want to look back at: the one where you spend all your time earning lots of money, or one where you were happy and lived your life to the fullest?
2. Have you ever really been happy in life and experienced true happiness?
3. What is that one thing that can cheer you up and make you happy, no matter how sad you are?
4. What are the three things you would always want for your family? Do you always allow yourself to have that or work on that?
5. What can hurt you the most in life?
6. How strongly do you want a life filled with happiness, enthusiasm and inner peace? Are you willing to take the efforts needed to get those?
7. Do you plan to choose yourself and your happiness above all, even when you're in the worst situations?
8. How have you been unfair to yourself and how do you plan to change that?

50 WAYS TO BE HAPPY

A. Self- realisation

1. Love

Love is the easiest way to be happy on an everyday, permanent basis. Think of anything you love doing, like playing your favourite sport or eating your favourite food. What happens when you are doing that? You are happy. Every time you truly love something (it could be anything, it will always make you happy because loving always leads to happiness. That is why it's so important for us to love our life because if we don't love, we can never really be happy with it. Loving our life will not only make us feel happy, excited, alive and give us peace of mind, but will also lead us to loving our surroundings, our job and the people in it.

This is why just being around certain people or meeting them makes us so happy. And what happens when you meet someone you don't like? Well, I don't need to spell that out for you, I can already see your eyes rolling. If you truly hate or dislike someone, just looking at their face or meeting them can spoil your entire day.

Most people are unhappy because they focus on the negatives in their life. As a result, they start complaining more and more about it and, before they realise, they start hating their job, their friends, their education and they start living a very unhappy life. Hence, we need to change our focus in life from hate to love, and from negative to positive.

This can be done by admiring people and adapting their good qualities, finding our life to be beautiful and meaningful, and loving everything around us – despite its faults – because the more we love, the happier we will be. The happier we will be, the more we will attract everything good to us and start to feel great about everything we come across. Life will start giving us more reasons to be happy. Good things will start happening to us and our life will be truly transformed.

But to love your life, you have to first love yourself. Remember, it all always starts within you. You can only give others what you truly have and feel within. And you can only learn to love by loving. So love yourself to that extent that when someone compliments you, you take it as an additional affirmation, not a revelation. The truth is that no one can make you happy until you are happy with yourself.

This is another reason why people are so happy when they start having feelings for someone or loving them. They just can't stop smiling and they start finding everything around them beautiful because it makes them love themselves and their life. Love makes everything beautiful and worth living. We all wish to find someone who can truly love us and make us happy. But why wait for someone else to make us happy and give us all that love? Let's resolve to be that person for ourselves and make self-love, self-appreciation and being happy our topmost priority.

2. Gratitude

The feeling of being grateful or thankful for whatever we have in our life is called gratitude. It is one of the simplest ways of being happy, regardless of the conditions or situations we face. Regardless of which country we are in, how much we earn or what we do in life, there is still so much for us to be thankful for. In life, no one has it all, not even the richest. But we can be thankful for everything God has given us and for all the love and blessings that are still coming our way.

Showing gratitude is simply about seeing the best in every situation, no matter how bad it is, like those who don't have a bike, they can be grateful they have two good legs to walk on; those who want to travel the world, but don't have enough money, can be grateful that they can see every corner of the world with a click of a button; those who don't have their own house can at least be happy about the fact that they have a shelter over their head and they are not on the streets.

So, in life, no matter what we have or don't have, we will always have something to be thankful for and as long as we choose to see the best in everything life throws at us, be it good or bad, nothing and no one can stop us from being happy. However, to be grateful, we need to leave the bad habits of complaining and self-loathing behind because doing that will only make us more unhappy and ungrateful about everything. But by practising gratitude, we will always ensure that we are attracting more goodness our way and that we are on the right track with the universe.

However, how can someone be grateful about something as horrible as accidents, diseases and deaths? I'll tell you how. If your kid has a disease, even the deadliest one, you're going to be very stressed and worried about it and you may have been grieving and praying and doing everything in your power to make it go away. However, being grateful about the fact that you at least found out about it in time and it can still be cured is something which can give you hope and let you be positive, even in the worst situation.

Point is, life is never constant. It keeps throwing problems and bad situations our way. However, that is not something that we can control; what we can control is how to deal with that. So let's stop focusing on our problems because no matter how big the problem is, dealing with it in a calm, composed and orderly manner, and being grateful that your problem isn't as bad as it could be will ensure that we stay positive, happy and have gratitude at all times in life.

3. Hope

Hope is the one thing that still helps us believe in the goodness of the world and people, and helps us hold onto our values and beliefs, even when it might not always be easy. Living in a world that is filled by social media, news channels, and newspapers, we all know where the country is headed and how many bad things are happening around us including rapes, acid attacks, murders, corruption, and the controversies never end. And when we step out in the real world, we come across heartbreaks, betrayal, gossip, etc.

So the truth is, living in a world like that may not always be easy - you would know, based on your own experiences. However, having hope, believing that there are good people out there, knowing that true love does exist and the world is not as bad as we think, helps us work towards a better future and stay happy in the long run.

Hope is the one thing that keeps us going and helps us stay motivated, even in tough times. It also helps us manage our stress, anxiety and trust issues. A hopeful person chooses to look at the positive side of everything, hence believes and sees the best in everyone. In life, bad things and bad situations happen to everyone. However, it is extremely important to not let those bad things get to us, by holding onto our ethical values and beliefs. A hopeful person is always someone closer to living a happy life.

Therefore, never let the hope within you die because when you hope, you start believing, and what we truly believe manifests in our life. So you're creating magic in your life and bringing happiness and prosperity towards you by just being someone with an innocent heart and a hopeful future. In a world full of darkness, having hope is like lighting a candle in our heart; this not only makes the darkness go away, but also helps us see the light and guides the rest of our journey. So go live a hopeful happy life. We all deserve it.

4. Purpose

As kids, our life's major purpose was to eat, sleep, smile, look cute and do that all over again. And as much as we loved that life and want to go back to it again, as we grow old, a lot of questions start emerging in our minds. These questions are majorly about our life, our visions, our purpose and what we truly want life to give us. Well, everyone tries finding their answers in life at some point or another in different ways. While some get them, some choose to live in the uncertainty.

However, we are born on this earth, at this particular time, in this specific era, for a purpose. As much as we want to believe that we are a result of some mistake done years ago, that is not the case. We are all here for some ultimate good with a purpose in our life. While everyone's reason to live, their talents and abilities, and that one thing that gives their life a purpose, are different, there is one thing common in all of us – whenever we find our purpose, it always leads us to our happiness.

Finding your purpose in life means finding those things that we are the most passionate about, which add meaning to our lives, make you happy no matter how many times you do it. We are all good at something in life. Some of us know our talents and while some stay ignorant. However, there are so many things and talents we can learn along our journey to make it more exciting and adventurous.

There is only one definite way of finding our purpose in life and that is by following our heart and achieving all our dreams. If you're in a job or in a field which does not excite you or make you jump out of your bed in the morning, you should know that you're in the wrong lane. Being in a place like that will only drain your energy and make you more unhappy. Take some time out, go on a vacation, get to know yourself and your abilities and find what you want to do and what your purpose in life is. There is never a right time to find the right things about your life and be happy.

It is a known fact that someone who follows their passion and finds their purpose in life is happier and much more motivated to live the life of their dreams and enjoy life to the fullest. Hence, it is extremely important to find your purpose in life because it will ultimately lead you to have a happy life in the long run. If you know it already, then follow it, and if you don't, then go find it and find yourself amongst all the chaos in your life. Yes, you are worthy of happiness; yes you are worthy of love; yes, you are worthy of every good thing coming to you;

and yes, you are worthy of a fantastic life with no regrets to look back on. So go live the life of your dreams. Now is your moment. Go seize it.

5. Stay calm and composed

In life, we all have our moments where we are triggered, cornered and filled with anger and resentment. This normally happens when things don't go as planned, people don't behave the way we want them to or we have high expectations from something. The outcome of that is usually one that we regret later, like saying things we don't mean, being rude, getting violent or filling our minds with negativity and enmity. Anger and hatred do not do anyone any good. It generally hurts us physically, emotionally, mentally and spoils our health. It also affects our relationship with other people.

We all know this, however, most of us still react adversely at the slightest of things because we don't know how to stay calm and composed. A person who is calm and composed is normally the one who does not react on instinct, controls their reactions and stays extremely positive in life, regardless of changing situations. Staying calm and composed is so important for us in life that its true meaning cannot be explained in words. It helps us to connect with the centre of our being and finding our true self.

It guides us to think more rationally, make correct decisions and find our peace of mind, thus, letting us be happy, irrespective of the things happening around us.

It gives us a chance to self-evaluate our words and actions, and turn them into situations best suitable for our growth. To be happy in life, we consciously need to stop letting situations and people control our reactions. We cannot control what someone else says or does, but we can control how we react to that and how much we let this affect us.

By dealing with things in a calmer composed manner, we are not only saving those many moments of happiness, but we start dealing with the situations in our lives in a much mature manner, saving a lot of melodrama, heartbreaks and lifelong relationships. We also truly start understanding the people around us and feel content with our life. We start being happier and more carefree. With nothing and no one pulling us back, we fight to start flying like a butterfly, spreading its wings and displaying its colours to the universe. Everyone loves being around someone who is so much fun, and full of life and happiness.

So by staying calm and composed, you are not only adding value to your life but also to the people around you. However, it might not always be easy to stay in that state of mind with so much happening around us. For that, you can meditate, be more positive, start being happier, learn to let go of things and start finding your true self. Imagine how powerful a person could be if he/she is not affected by the external world and just focuses on their inner bliss. Well, it's about time we are that person.

6. Stop connecting happiness with success or more money

For most of us, happiness is something that can be attained when we are successful, or when we have a big bank account or have more materialistic things. Hence, we buy things we feel add value to our life like a brand-new car, a bigger house or more luxuries, hoping it will bring us immediate happiness and gratification. When that doesn't happen, we buy more and more, only to be disappointed once again. As a result of that, no one is really happy because no matter how much we have, it's never enough. After all, our greed always gets ahead of us and there will always be someone else who will have more than us.

Well, happiness is not something that you can buy and it is not something you can ever really lose. Think of anything you wanted for a long time and how did you feel when you got that? Well, of course, you must have been very happy when you got that and you must have clicked pictures and posted it on social media, but how long did that happiness last? Did getting something you wanted and worked so hard for make you happy forever, or was that happiness just temporary? In life, do you want to stay happy only in certain moments or do you want to stay happy forever?

Well, a lifetime of happiness is not found in something that can be paid for; it's within you. You have the power to make yourself happy in every moment you live, you just have to choose to be happy. So, we need to stop running behind things and be happy with what we have and start celebrating life. To be truly happy, we need to stop waiting for moments to make us happy, start creating beautiful moments for ourselves, and appreciate and value the small things that can add so much meaning in our life.

True happiness is happiness inside you. It is enjoying your own company and living in love and peace with your body, mind and soul. Happiness is not about what we get but it's truly about what we give. It is found in simple things like watching the birth of a baby, playing with your pet, listening to your favourite song or spending time with your family.

Most of us use our problems, circumstances or our conditions as an excuse to be unhappy. Well, let me break this to you: it doesn't matter if you have financial problems at home, or a bad relationship, or you don't have the lifestyle you want, because as much as this affects us and how we feel, we can choose to be above that and be happy. Stop waiting for everything to be perfect, start now. Just smile from your heart and be happy, excited and crazy about everything. Love your imperfections, love yourself and the life you have built, and happiness will follow.

7. Find out what makes you happy

Many people think that happiness is about having fun at a party, the excitement of new experiences and adventure, the delight of an amazing meal or the thrill and passion for a newfound love. They are all wonderful experiences to be cherished but that is not happiness; they are pleasures. And as much fun as we have at that moment, it is short-lived. Pleasure is a temporary experience such as food, sex, and shopping. Hence, chasing after pleasure is not happiness, at least not for a very long time.

Therefore, we cannot live our life being dependent on temporary experiences, external factors, people or situations to make us feel great about our self. We need to be enough for our self and we need to find our happiness. But do we always know what makes us happy? The answer is no. This is because as we change or grow as a person, our thinking, the way we see the world and how things affect us starts to change. Due to this, our sources of happiness also change. Like, for example, getting small chocolates as a kid can make you happy, but that might not always make you happy as you grow up, and you might need more than that to find happiness.

So finding your happiness is not a one-time thing. It is something you have to do all your life. But how do you find your happiness? How ever much you change, whichever version of yourself you grow up to be, the ultimate way to find a lifetime of happiness is by being in the moment and enjoying it to the fullest, even if you're not doing anything great or special. You are investing your time and effort by being there, so why not get the most out of it? Well, everyone finds happiness differently. But whichever way you find happiness, it is always accompanied by love, for happiness is ultimately the love of life, the celebration of giving, and loving and smiling your way through life.

Most of us get so busy in our daily lives that we forget the importance of small moments in life, like watching your kid win his first trophy, playing with your pet, watching a mother hold her newborn baby. They are all wonderful experiences that happen to us or the people around us. Live these simple moments. Find joy in someone else's happiness. Celebrate how far you have come in life and how far you dream to go. Smile even on your toughest days. Spend time with yourself and love yourself each day that you live.

It is not difficult, finding happiness, if you can find it in everything around you. Look around you: isn't everything around you beautiful? Unique but useful, and valuable in its way. Now look at you and your beautiful hands, your lovable heart and your sweet smile; you are a masterpiece: an extraordinary person who deserves everything good in life. Feel the love in your being and pass it to everybody around you. Smile at strangers, help the needy and greet everyone you come across. Finding happiness is not hard. It's within you, it's around you and it's near you, always. All you have to do is let yourself feel it.

8. We can control only two things: our attitude and our effort

In life, knowingly or unknowingly, we expect so much from people. Even though this is very normal, this can sometimes really hurt us. These expectations could be based on how close they are to us and what we expect them to do, like stand by us, support us, be there for us when we are low, etc. We expect people to treat us or love us the way we treat them, though that might not always be fair. We cannot expect someone to be as generous, as loving or as thoughtful as we are. People will see, do and understand things from their level of thinking and as much as we want to argue with that, it is just a reality we need to accept.

Hence, having a lot of expectations of how a certain moment should go or how someone should be leads to disappointment because, when things don't go like that, not only do we get disappointed and unhappy but we also cannot enjoy the moment for what it is. So, to be happy, don't expect anything from anyone because then even the small effort the person takes will make you happy. It is a much simpler and happier way of living. Do what you feel is right and take efforts where you think you should because you can't control what someone else does anyway. Just focus on you and be happy.

However, our attitude is another thing which can stop us from attaining happiness. In life, our attitude defines everything. It is those frames that you wear on your eyes through which you see the world. If you have a positive attitude in life, you will find the good in everything, regardless of how good or bad it is. But if you have a negative approach to life, you will find faults in everything and live a very unhappy life. Your attitude is your perception of the world, so make sure it's beautiful because it will make your life that way.

Therefore it is important to have an approach which facilitates your growth, makes you see the greatness in everything and drives you to do crazy things. To have a happy healthy life, develop good thoughts, let go of negativity, appreciate everything you come across and stop letting other people and their actions take away your peace of mind. You have come a long way, but you still have a long way to go. But you don't have to do this alone, let me walk with you through this journey and, step-by-step, we will reach our destination.

9. Contentment and peace of mind

We all want to look back on a life that we will be proud of, where we were crazy, lived fully and laughed enormously. Looking back at a happy life when we are 90 is each person's dream. But how many of us are working towards living that life? Somewhere, we get so caught up in our daily schedule that we forget how necessary it is to just sit back and enjoy with our loved ones, or do something crazy and spontaneous without thinking about it twice. We are so full of responsibilities that stress has become our daily companion.

From taking care of our family to keeping our boss happy, from completing our assignments to getting good grades, we are all pressurized to do well in life no matter what age we are. The constant pressure to be better than everyone else and build a successful life keeps us so preoccupied that we forget how important it is to feel content and find a piece of ourselves in everything we do.

Feeling content is about living life feeling satisfied and fulfilled. It is about enjoying our journey no matter how many times we slip or fall, and celebrating each step along the way. It is a constant state of mind we need to be in for us to be happy. To be content in life, don't expect too much; accept things for what they are, believe in the greater good and know that everything in life happens for a reason. Just trust the universe with where it's guiding you.

A person who is content is normally someone who is happy in life and finds their peace of mind. Like, for instance, if you study in the field of your choice, despite its difficulties, everything about it will excite you and you will look forward to grasping more knowledge. Being there in that college, in that field, with those professors and friends, will start to be fun. You will feel content and find your happiness by just being there, and you will naturally reach that state where you find peace of mind.

Finding peace of mind can help you grow spiritually, and deal with things in a much simpler and calmer manner. It can enhance your view of the world and align your thoughts in a way that they will bring you maximum benefit. A lot of people travel the world, go to ashrams, do meditation, go trekking and isolate themselves from the world to find themselves and their inner peace. All I can say is, seeking contentment and finding your peace of mind is a wonderful journey, and the

the sooner you get it, the less the noise of the world will matter. Feel so complete within that everything outside you is just a reflection of that.

10. Do what's right, not what's easy

Since childhood, we are all taught to do the right thing and differentiate between right and wrong. For instance, hitting someone was a bad thing but sharing with someone was always a good deed. Our parents repeatedly told us the right thing to do to get that kind of behaviour from us. But as we grow older, that thin line between right and wrong gets fainter. We start deciding on our own what's right and what is best for us.

We feel like we know what we are doing and getting into, and we can take care of our self. But that doesn't always happen, does it? We do things by being in the present, without thinking about its consequences for the future. That not only lands us in trouble but also initiates bad habits among us that affect us and our families. Hence, it is extremely important to make wise choices in life.

In life, no matter who we are, what we do, what our age is or how successful, we are faced with a constant choice - choice of doing the right thing. Though this may not always be easy, it is a decision that we make for ourselves that defines not only our actions in the present but also our behaviour in the future. Our decisions, no matter how small or big they are, are so crucial that they start framing our mind and attitude about things.

For instance, by finding shortcuts of doing your work or avoiding your work as much as you can, you are not only developing a casual attitude towards work but you are also running away from hard work and persistence. That will result in an unhappy boss, leading to an unhappy work condition and a bad mindset about you. Also, leading to you not being considered for promotions or taken seriously in your workplace, leading to a miserable unhappy life in the future.

So, as we can see, every decision we take has a crucial impact on our life. We often take wrong decisions thinking it's an easier way out and, before we realise it, we start developing bad thoughts that lead us to take the wrong actions and, ultimately, an unhappy life. A happy life can be achieved only by finding out what's right and making that decision for yourself, no matter how hard it is. So, if you want a better life, start making better life decisions from now on. Nothing you truly want will ever come easy, but I can say it will always be worth the effort.

B. Work on your relationships

1. Get rid of toxic people

In life, we want to be surrounded by people. These people may be the ones we know or the ones we are fond of and hang out with regularly. Regardless, our need to live a social life has increased. This could be due to the influence of social media, our need to belong somewhere or simply due to our ego and our inferiority complex. However, no matter how many people we are with, doesn't it matter what kind of people we are around?

The truth is, it does; the people who are around us constantly, like our friends and family, have a huge impact on us and on how we think, see things and what kind of a person we grow up to be. We cannot choose our family, they are gifted to us, but we can choose our friends and the people we get in a relationship with. They are those people in our life who we let in and trust the most. We open up to them about our vulnerabilities, we go to them when we have a problem, and they are often the ones who know the most about us.

They sometimes even know us better than ourselves. However, not every person we let in has the best intentions for us. Sometimes the people who are closest to us cause us the most harm. They hurt us and act in ways we never imagined. They portray a different picture in front of us but behind us, they are truly evil. The worst thing you can ever do to yourself is trusting someone who is only going to hurt you with a knife in your back and the worst lie will always be the one said to your face.

We, unknowingly, invite such people in our lives who only cause chaos. Even after we get to know their reality, we overlook such things because we love them and we want to forgive them and believe that they are better than that. We keep justifying their behaviour and our weakness towards them but, the truth is, such toxic people never deserve a place in our life. No matter how much we love them or give them, they are never going to be able to love us back the same way. So, holding onto such people will only cause more pain in our life.

It is essential to let them go for us to hold onto our self-worth. We need to know what we deserve and let go of everything that falls short of that. We need to put our self and our needs first, and cut-off anyone who does not facilitate our growth. Toxic people, toxic relationships and toxic friendships need to be discarded from our life for us to feel good. We need to focus on people who love us and stay with us, even in extreme difficulties. Remember, everything meant for you in life will always find its way back to you and stay, and everything else will just keep flowing with time. So don't try to make things work, sometimes it's necessary to leave them as what they are.

2. Spend quality time with your family

When we were kids, our world revolved around our parents. We found happiness and joy in them. But as we grew older and started meeting new people, we started being dependent on them for our happiness, like our new college friends, our work colleagues, and so on. We start investing so much time with them that there is hardly any left for our family. We are outside the whole day, we meet people, check their social media, get stuck in meetings, work our ass off, and come home and do the same things all over again.

We are so busy in making everyone else happy that we forget to keep those people happy whose world revolves around us. The value of our family is lost because they are always there for us, no matter what. It starts becoming so crucial for us to connect with the outside world that we forget to connect with ourselves and the people who love us the most. We also start becoming so ambitious as we grow that we forget the people who worked so hard to make all our dreams come true.

Our family is our everything; our rock, the reason behind our hard work and our happy place. No matter where we go, no matter how many mistakes we make or how much ever we fail in life, knowing that we can come home to someone who would always embrace us with open arms and love in their eyes is a gift beyond measure. The love and strength we get from our family is unconditional. Everyone has a home. For most people its four walls, but home is where the family is. That's where dreams dwell, sweat is mixed with happiness and efforts are matched by love.

So spend time with them, talk to them, laugh with them and love them unconditionally because, at the end of the day, family is all we have. That is why it's so important for us to cherish each and every moment we spend with them and start finding joy in simple things, like sleeping in our mother's lap, having a heart- to-heart discussion with our dad, and troubling our siblings and watching some old movies with them. The value of such simple moments cannot be measured. They have lived their entire lives trying to give us a good life, taking care of us and fulfilling our needs. Now, it's time we return the favour.

They never made excuses when we needed them, so let's not make excuses now when they need us. Practice simple habits like telling your parents you love them, spending some quality time with them and sharing everything with them. It might take only a few minutes but it will make their day. And what is better than the smile on your father's face and tears of happiness in your mother's? Can anything else be more beautiful in this world? Let's take more efforts to make sure their smiles never go away.

3. Find people who love for who you are

In life, we are constantly surrounded by people. Some faces are new, while some are old. Some friendships stay tight even after so many years, while some just fade away with time. Some people fight only to make up later, while some hold onto their grudges. Some people love unconditionally, while some stay around only for their needs. Some stay in our happy times and laugh with us, while some know us better than ourselves and cry for us. In life, we come across all kinds of people, but do all these people stay?

Well, not really. As time goes, everyone's priority keeps changing. People move on and get busy with their own lives. However, the only ones who stick around are the people who truly appreciate us, know our strengths as well as our faults, but still love us regardless. We spend so much of our time loving the wrong people and in dead-end relationships that we drain ourselves of happiness and of receiving anything good that comes to us.

True love never comes with conditions. It is about accepting people for who they are and not for who we want them to be. Everyone we meet has faults. Nobody in this world is perfect and no one is expected to be, but seeing someone beyond those imperfections is true beauty. Finding people in life who do not judge us, stand by us, support us and are always there for us is a true blessing.

These are the kinds of people who are with us through thick and thin. In life, we all need people who truly love us like our family and friends. We are most comfortable around such people because we do not fear being judged. The result of being around such people is always happiness. They have a huge impact on our self-growth. They not only motivate us to be the best versions of ourselves, but also help us in achieving greatness in life.

Therefore, it is extremely important for us to find people who love us for who we are. This helps us love and accept ourselves a little more. It brings meaning to our life and opens our doors to happiness. No one can ever grow in an unhappy or toxic environment. As a result, keep yourself surrounded by people who love you. Love fully and freely. Find your kind of people. Don't push them away and be that friend you look for in someone else. Who knows what kind of magic that will bring?

4. Make others happy with small acts of kindness

Most of us focus on our needs, wants and greed so much that we often forget those people who are blessed with no parents, have disabilities and bad financial conditions. These people have no homes, families and are faced with extremely bad conditions. As much as we want to believe that we have nothing to do with them, helping them and being there for them is an act of selflessness.

In life, we always get what we give. If we want to receive love, kindness, generosity and respect, then that's what we need to give to others. Similarly, if we wish to receive enormous amounts of wealth, then we need to give some of it away in forms of charity, social work and donations to people. In order to receive, we need to always give and leave the rest to karma. Hence, it's like a magnet: everything you give with a pure heart and a true conscience will always find its way back to you.

The universe has amazing ways in adding some spark to our life. God created this world; if he would have wanted, he could have made everyone healthy and wealthy, and then half the problems would be solved. However, he wanted to test us and our willingness to do something without getting anything in return, hence he created difficulties and bad conditions. He wanted us to learn the importance of sharing, humbleness, selflessness and love.

Doing something for others does not only make them happy but also makes us happy, and gets us enormous amounts of love and blessings in return. It doesn't take a lot to make someone happy. We don't necessarily always need money for that, we can do small acts of kindness by spending time with people in old age homes, teaching kids in orphanages and giving them old clothes and toys, giving food to people in need or doing a performance for cancer-ridden or disabled children to make them smile.

It is small steps like these that create a beautiful future for someone else and lead them to live a happy life. For us, money is everything and we worship it. But money still can't buy the happiness a small kid on the road feels when we buy him an ice cream or the happiness a street vendor feels when we buy from them under the scorching heat. For us, buying that is nothing, but, for them, it is the cost of keeping their family going. Hence, we should help others as much as we can. Find happiness in someone else's joy. Remember, money doesn't matter, efforts do. So, start now. Try changing a life and see the impact it has on your own.

5. Create a positive environment at home

It is often said that a child's mind starts developing right from its mother's womb. The impact of a mother's thought process, frame of mind, attitude and habits are often seen in a new-born baby. Similarly, as time goes by and the child starts growing up, it starts adapting everything it is taught, like its relationship with others, words and sentences taught by us, and the various do's and don'ts. The impact of the environment at home can be seen very evidently from the birth of a baby till the time we grow old.

Our basic mind frame, our values and our perception of the world depends upon what is taught to us from our childhood or what we see happening around us. Later, we start growing our own mind and start questioning everything as we grow. However, a good upbringing and a positive environment have a very good impact on our life. It helps us become a strong, independent person with good morals and ethics. It helps us stay happy and gives us the support we need. It helps us generate a lot of positive memories about our childhood and pushes us to achieve greatness in life.

Whereas, creating a negative environment at home due to fights, disagreements, illness or physical abuse can lead to everyone being very unhappy in the family. It will lead to stress, depression, anger and resentment amongst each other. The kids are often traumatized in such circumstances and it has a huge impact on their mind.

The kids growing in such homes are often troubled and it creates a very negative environment for anyone to come home to or live in.

Hence, the kind of environment we create at home does not only affect us but it also affects our family. That is why creating a positive environment at home is so necessary. Laugh, talk, share and spend time with your parents. It will lead to manifestation of happiness on an everyday basis. It may not always be easy to create a positive environment due to prevailing circumstances, but start with yourself. Stay happy and try to make everyone around you happy.

Our family is everything to us. It is our reason for happiness as well as our reason to live. We all want to see our close and loved ones happy. So why not take efforts to make them happy, tell them we love them and give them the love and care they deserve? Creating a positive environment at home is as important as being happy in life because we grow where we are planted. If the soil we are grown in is not good, it will never lead to a fruitful life. In order to be happy, regardless of everything happening around us, we must choose to be above that. Make your family as happy as they wish to make you.

6. Make new friends

No matter who we are or what age we are in, we always keep coming across new people. Everywhere we go, we are surrounded by new faces and those are the number of chances we have towards making new friends. Honestly, those chances are endless. We make friends in school, and then we go to college, meet new people there and make crazy memories with them, and then we either find a job or start something on our own and meet new people there all over again.

The people around us are never common. In every phase of life, every new class we join or probably every new trip we take, we make so many new friends, we come across so many different people and form so many different bonds. With time, some bonds just fade away or their value is lost, while we meet some people who feel like we've known them forever.

Friends are our lifeline. They spend time with us, make us laugh, stand by us and even make us cry. They are the people who push us to do new things and live life to the fullest. They make us do the craziest things and do the stupidest pranks on us. The memories we make with them are countless, our craziness with them is limitless, and the inside jokes with them are endless. They are our extended family and it is honestly difficult to survive in this world without true friends.

However, no matter how many people we know or how many friends we have, it is very important for us to step out of our safety net and make conversations with new people and invite them in our lives. It is like bungee-jumping from a mountain and not knowing where you will fall. It's crazy, exciting and adventurous, but it is fun. When we talk to new people, we don't know where they are from, what they do, what they like or even what kind of life they live. There is so much to talk about and so much to learn from them.

So be kind, honest and friendly to people and life will gift you a lot of friends. But more than that, you will have so many experiences to learn from and so many people to look forward to. Thereby, open your heart out to the world and it will be filled with love, compassion and kindness. The strongest friendships I have heard have started in the most random ways. So do random things and find the Joey to your Chandler, the Peyton to your Brooke, and the Sonu to your Titu because honestly, it's never too late to make new friends and to start living.

7. Love yourself

We spend so much of our time focusing on others, their lives and loving them, that we often forget about our self. No matter how much we try fixing the world, it will not be fixed until something within us is healed. We walk in this world with a broken heart and then blame others for our problems. All our life and relationship problems, knowingly or unknowingly, started from us. Everything we wish to find in this world is within us and all we need to do is look.

It is said that we can only give others what we truly have or feel from within. That is why it is so important for us to love our self because until we don't, we can never really love the world. What we feel from within is more important than what we show others. We have so many unresolved issues and so many things that hinder us from within that we don't realise those things have an impact on every relationship we make.

Whenever we have a fight with someone, we apologize to them, show them that we care and make efforts to make it okay. However, we never take the same efforts for our self. We never tell our self that it is okay to make mistakes or be wrong sometimes. In this world we give our self the harshest treatment. We constantly judge our self and how we are behaving, we shout at our self, get mad and leave it at that. We never ever forgive our self or let things go.

That is the biggest reason why we have so many issues with others because we never really resolved them within us. It is easy to run from the world but how can we run from our self? The things we did will eventually catch up to us. But what is also true is that we need to spend time with our self, indulge in self-care, love and nourish our soul. We need to accept our self the way we are. We spend so much of our time fighting with our self and thinking about how we are expected to be, that we never really accept who we really are.

Until we don't accept who we are, we will never be able to love our self fully and if we can't love our self, we can't expect others to. The void in our heart can only be fulfilled by us. No one can come and make us fall in love with our self, because that's our job. We need to love our self enough to take a stand for us. We need to love our self enough to know what we deserve and to put our self and our needs as a priority, and let go of anyone who cannot match up to that. We are enough for our self. We always were and we always will be because, at the end of the day, our love and our acceptance is all we need to stay happy.

8. Everyone has an opinion of you

Everyone sees us differently. This is because we behave differently with different people. We don't behave crazily in front of everyone, go on talking rubbish for hours together, share everything happening in our personal lives, or show how sad we feel. We don't open up to everyone and, as a result, everyone has varying images in their heads of who we are. While some think of us as talkative, some think we are quiet, while some go on to think we have so much of attitude and ego, and the list goes on.

It is actually funny how different people think so differently of the same person. It doesn't matter if that person knows us or not, or if we have ever talked to them earlier, or how strong a bond we share with them, because everyone has an opinion of us. It may not always be one that we may like or approve of, but it's there and there is nothing we can do about it. Honestly, we also have an opinion about everyone, even if we may not know them.

Living in an era where people judge before knowing us, and what people think of us is more important than who we are, this has a great impact on us, even if we don't show it. We want to be in everyone's good books and we want everyone to love us. As nice as that sounds, that never happens. There are always people who have a problem with us. However, that should not affect us or pull us back.

What people think of us is their reality, not ours. Sometimes, in order to prove we are not that person, we end up becoming someone exactly like that. Therefore, in order to be happy, stop letting other people's opinions and what they think and talk about affect you so much because we know who we are and what the truth is - and that's what matters. We don't owe anyone any explanation.

The more we focus on what they say, the closer we are towards becoming that person as that's what we start focusing on. So, know yourself and focus on positive things. People can only affect us if we let them. Stop letting people get to you. Be stronger than that. Focus on your happiness and inner peace and everything else will fall into place. Let people misunderstand, lie or assume things about us because there will come a day when they see who we really are. Until then, accept yourself so well that no matter what someone else says, it does not make a difference.

9. Be there for others in times of need

We all wish to have people in our lives who will be there for us in times of need. These are the people we trust the most and share our personal lives with. These are the people who are there for us always. Honestly, handling everything on our own can be very stressful and tiring. We all need a shoulder to cry on, a friend to talk to and a warm hug to embrace us at the end of a bad day. However, we sometimes get so lost and confused that we need to be correctly guided into doing the right thing.

Therefore, have no fear in admitting that we don't always know the right thing to do. Have no fear in admitting that we all need someone at the end of the day. As a matter of fact, everyone does need someone else regardless of how strong we are and this is not our weakness, but our strength. This dependency is what makes human relationships so beautiful because if we didn't need someone's help or didn't support each other, the earth would have turned into an unending battlefield. Love unites us all and makes us humble.

As a result, as much as we need others, others need us too. Sometimes in ways we cannot imagine. Being there for people in their times of need does not only make us a good person but also makes us happy. Being there for someone in their pain, grief or problems not only helps us know what is going on in their lives but gives them the strength to come out of that. Listening to someone's problems does not just help us to give them the correct advice but it also helps them to empty their mind of negativity. Helping someone who cannot help themselves like the poor or needy, does not only get us blessings and good wishes but also helps us in living a life knowing we have done someone some good. That we lived a life making others happy.

Everything that we do for others has a way of helping us and making us happy. How much we give is how much we receive. Hence, all the happiness we need can be received by making others happy. The best smile is one that can be seen on someone else's face because of us. It is honestly the best feeling in the world. The only good we have done is where we expected nothing in return. It is living a life of selflessness, humility and pure love.

At the end of the day, it didn't matter how many people looked at us and smiled, but what matters is how many smiles we brought on others' faces. It doesn't matter how much we earned but how much we spent to make someone else's life better. It doesn't matter how many people were there for us when we needed them, but what matters is how many people were we there for when they needed us. A person's life is summarised by not what they achieve but how they spend what they achieve and what good they do to the world.

10. Life is the sum of our experiences

We go through various phases in life, right since we are born. As kids, our major problem was getting our homework done and getting good marks in exams and that is what we focused on back then. But as adults, our problems can be way more complex than that, both emotionally and financially. With each experience that we go through, we have something to look back on, something to cherish, something to remember and something to learn from. Our life is never a straight-line. It is like the graph on the machine monitoring heartbeats - filled with its ups and downs. It never lets us stay comfortable in one place and no time, be it good or bad, lasts forever.

It teaches us a lesson to look beyond bad times and know that good days will come soon. It teaches us to look beyond those good days and be prepared to face the bad days as well. Our life can be compared to morning and night. No matter how bright the sun shines in the morning, in the evening it has to go down and no matter how dark it is at night, the sun will shine again. This not only gives us hope for better days but also teaches us a greater lesson. No matter what problem we are in, it won't last forever.

So, just hold on and let the bad times sail away. Face everything with utmost dignity and a smile, because if we recall our life up till now, it will be the things we have done, the experiences we've gone through and the people we have lived it with. Everyone's life can be summarised like this regardless of the fact that you are the president of America or a normal worker earning their daily wage. Our life is the sum total of our experiences. If we had good experiences until now then we lived a good life but if we had bad experiences, then we lived a bad life.

So, if at any point of time we want to change our life then we have to change our experiences. We can change our experiences by making good decisions and we can make good decisions by rational thinking. Hence, we need to think through the decision we are taking and the impact it will have on us and our lives. Most decisions we take, happen in the spur of the moment without thinking of its end result and such decisions often have a way of firing back at us. We need to be more careful of what we invite into our life.

We need to see everything in terms of its pros and cons. In order to live a happy life, we need to create happy situations around us. Start looking for experiences which facilitate self-growth. Do things which bring us closer to our self and our peace of mind. Choose to be happy in every moment we live. Let go of things that hold us back. Life is not complicated; we make it that way. Being happy isn't difficult either, it's simply a choice to put our self and our happiness first in every moment we live. Don't just let life pass away, make the most of it in every moment we live because honestly this life is all we got.

C. Focus on feeling good in every moment

1. Live in present

The reason most people are unhappy is because they still hold onto the past and holding onto our past is like holding a hot iron; it always hurts. No matter how many times we have been hurt before or how long we hold onto it, it never gets better, the pain only gets deeper and deeper. "If I would have said this, then this would have happened and then she would have said this and this could have been avoided". Well, that didn't happen the way we wanted it to and now it never will. We have to know that and we have to make peace with that.

None of us have the choice of changing our past, no matter how good or bad it is. The only thing we can do is accept it and make amends to make our future better. There are so many problems in people's lives, so many issues, there is so much we hold onto that the weight of all that gets us down. Most of us are filled with guilt, regrets and disappointments and we run that in an endless loop in our minds. We focus so much on what could have been that we forget what we have right now. We are so stuck up in our past that we fail to enjoy every moment we live.

We expect so much out of every moment that when things don't happen the way we planned them we often stay disappointed. As humans we all make mistakes, be it a child or a 70-year-old grown man. There is still so much for all of us to learn and honestly if we did everything right in the first go, we wouldn't really learn. Then, we would simply think that we are God or someone extraordinary. The fact that we make mistakes and then correct them, makes us humble. The fact that learning is a never-ending process, helps us grow in life. The fact that we still have so much to look forward to helps us live and enjoy every moment.

The only way we can live and enjoy every moment we have, is by living in the present and the only way of living in the present is by not staying in our past or worrying too much about our future. Both of them give us no good but stress and disappointments. Being too anxious to create a good future often ruins our present. We start focusing so much on what we would be after 5 years or 10 or after our retirement that we often forget the importance of the moment we are living in.

Therefore, we need to focus only on our present. When we live in the present, we make the most of everything we have. We stay happy, content and have our peace of mind. We are in a state where we are closest to our inner self. We start living life in complete satisfaction and are free of any worries or stress. If we really want to be happy, we need to let go of our past and not worry too much about our future in order to truly create a beautiful life in our present.

2. Focus on health and well-being

As humans, our major objective is earning lots of money to buy things that we consider important. However, in the process of earning lots and lots of money we start working too hard and push ourselves so much that our health is always compromised. In the priority list of things, we consider our health somewhere towards the end though it is one of the most important things we need in order to survive and the only time we actually pay attention to it is when something happens and we fall sick.

As kids we play and run around carelessly, not scared to get hurt. As young adults when we play any rough sport like football or hockey, we often get hurt but that never stops us because we never take our injuries seriously. We do rigorous gymming to get in shape without thinking of the impact it has on our body and the injuries we are causing it. We drive while talking on the phone and we often keep working when we fall sick and the list can go on. Lord knows how much we neglect our health.

That is exactly why we need to change our outlook and we need to start focusing on our health and well-being. We need to give our body the rest and the importance it deserves. Passion towards something is great, it makes us feel alive but as much as we feel that we are strong, we don't need rest and that we can fight our illness, continuing with our lives, the truth is that we need to take care of our body. We need to love our body because it's very tender. We need to protect our body from any external harm and take constant care of it because if we don't, we are destined to lead a very unhappy and unhealthy life.

How do we feel when we are sick with fever or any other illness or disease? We feel weak, unhappy, undesirable or low. No one is ever happy with a sickness. Have we ever heard someone say 'Thank God I got this illness or disease. I am so happy with it' or 'I am so grateful to be unwell, something good is going to come out of it'? Being unhealthy leads us to being unhappy and the more unhealthy we are, the more unhappy and sad life will end up being. Bad health takes a lot from us, our friends, family and our happiness. Hence, in order to live a happy life, we need to take care of our self and our close ones.

Do you know who our real best friend is? It's our body. It's the one person in life that would never leave us till the end. It fights for us, cures us and understands us but in return we only need to take care of it and nurture our body, mind and soul. We need to take our injuries seriously. We need to eat right and give our self a rest every once in a while. We need to be as safe as we can because the moment our body gives up on us, we will have nothing to fight for because we wouldn't even live. So, let's care for our body, the way it takes care of us.

3. Change your focus in life

Our life is a result of our thoughts. What we think is what we say and it is exactly what we end up doing. So, if we really want to change our life, we need to first change our thinking and monitor our thoughts. Now, a normal human being has on an average, 60,000 thoughts in a day. It is not humanly possible for us to control each of these thoughts or monitor them or even as a matter of fact, have all good thoughts in a day. We naturally have some negative thoughts about things we see or about what is happening around us and that is okay.

However, we can try to end our negative thoughts with positive ones. Like suppose, we come across some dish we don't like, we will end up criticizing it but, in the end, we can acknowledge the effort it took for someone to make it. Or if someone makes a mistake it will naturally get us pissed but at the end of the day, we can forgive them and move on. We don't realise the importance of this but what we think and give out in the universe is exactly what comes back to us in different ways.

So, if we are stuck in a problem instead of focusing so much on the problem and making it look so big, we can actually change our focus and look towards the solution. That way, not only will we get out of a problem but we will also find an appropriate solution. This works in all our areas of life. We have all heard the famous saying, '*What we sow is what we reap*', similarly, what we focus on is exactly what we get in life.

So, if we really want to be happy in life but all we are thinking about is how unhappy we are and how many bad things keep happening to us, then we are attracting more of that to our self and we will stay unhappier because all our thoughts are about how unhappy we are. Life will bring us more situations which will make us unhappier. Hence, if we really want to be happy in life, we need to stop focusing on the bad things going on in our life and actually change our focus to the good things we still have in our life. That way we will not only have something to be happy about but we would also be attracting more good things to our self.

The universe is like a mirror. What you show in the mirror through your thoughts is exactly what we get in life situations, people and circumstances. For most people, being happy is not easy. It could be one of the most expensive things because they feel they don't deserve happiness or there is a list of things they have to complete in order to be happy. However, happiness is simply about enjoying every moment and being carefree and by changing our focus from negative to positive things in life, we are already closer to having a lifetime of happiness.

4. Bask in the simple pleasures

Our life is what we make it. A person with a positive attitude, who chooses to look at the best of everything and finds delight in small moments, generally ends up living a very happy life. While a person who is constantly focused on their problems and stresses out a lot, tends to have a more unhappy life. We make everything around us so complicated. We overthink, over analyse and try to make sense of everything we come across. Most people live their lives in confusion. Feelings of being lost, emptiness and loneliness often surround us.

We spend our entire life trying to find its meaning when it is always right in front of us. Life is not about the big or the historic moments we try to make that can be written down in history. It's about simple living and finding happiness in the smallest of things and moments. It's about dancing with your friends on a rainy day, having ice-cream with your kids in summer and having a cup of hot coffee by yourself on a winter day.

Life is about being happy in all seasons, in all months and all days that we live. Happiness is found in simple things like watching the glorious sunset, or spending a wonderful evening with our family or hanging out with our friends in a café, laughing about stupid things. These are our most cherished moments and our life is a collection of these small moments. So, it's these small moments we need to enjoy the most. However, most of us feel like we have to do something to be happy.

As a reader, you're spending your time reading this book right now and trying to get something out of it, find happiness in that, in this exact moment. It's not easy being happy 24/7 with our complicated lives but we can try finding happiness in simple things and bask in the simple pleasures of life. The richest man is not the happiest man on earth. The happiest man on earth is someone who chooses to be happy despite what happens with them.

Every situation we are stuck in, every situation that we feel unhappy in, we can do two things about it. Either we can sit and keep complaining or frown about it or realise we are stuck there no matter what, so at least be happy in it. Everyone says happiness is a choice, well it's our choice. It's a choice we make every time we feel happy. A moment of pride in a parent's eyes, a beautiful time spent with loved ones or getting our first salary. We all know what these moments feel like, yet like sand they slip away and we never allow our self to have more of them. That's what we need to change. We need to let ourselves be free and happy. We need to believe that we deserve to be happy because when we believe in that, we are choosing to be happy.

5. Affective forecasting

Our life is never constant. No situation, no matter how good it is, can stay constant in our life. Life keeps presenting us with problems and circumstances we constantly have to deal with. Just when we think everything is okay, something else pops up and this is a never-ending process. Our life is a beautiful mixture of problems and solutions, tension and relief, love and loneliness, uniformity and growth, stress and relief, smiles and tears and day and night.

Every good phase in our lives comes to an end and we are faced with an even greater difficulty and challenge in our hands. Life therefore is somewhat like a video game. With every level we clear, we learn something new and grow but the game does not end there. Life keeps presenting us with new obstacles, to make our journey and our success even more fun. With everything that we pass through, we feel like we have achieved something; we feel strength, happiness, joy and it prepares us for whatever is coming ahead.

While we may not always know what is going to come in front of us when we are driving this journey of life, we can, however, always prepare ourselves by anticipating our hindrances or problems beforehand. This is known as affective forecasting. It simply means anticipating our problems beforehand based on changing circumstances. This helps us to deal with things or situations in a better way as we already had an idea that it was going to happen so we get a chance to prepare or respond to things in a better way.

Affective forecasting however, may not help us deal with all our problems as life can still give us the hardest blows and throw us off our A game at any point of time. But it can make things easier by helping us deal with a response to things we already anticipated. This way we are readier to face whatever life throws at us and we are not caught off guard. This also helps us stay emotionally stronger, move forward and to deal with small or big problems in life very effectively.

To apply this to our day-to-day lives, we have to observe our surroundings closely and find various remedies to deal with changing circumstances. Try thinking of all the problems we can have when we start something and solve them even before they arise. This way, half our problems would already be gone and we'd stay happy all the time as this allows us to maintain a stable state of mind and lets us be happy even in bad conditions. Just think about it; how sorted and peaceful would our life be if we already knew all the problems we were going to have because then we would most likely deal with things in a much better manner and stay happier.

6. Help others with compassion and generosity through social work

We are all very fortunate that we have been born in good families with good health and upbringing and that

God has blessed us enough for us to have whatever we want in life. We have so much to be grateful for in our life and yet we keep crying and running after things we can't have. We spend most of our lives focusing on our self, on our needs and on what we want such that we often forget about those who have no one to take care of them or are not blessed with enough resources to survive.

Now we don't know them personally and as a result we don't owe them anything but still it is our responsibility to take care of each other and help each other grow as a society. As a human being, it is our duty to help those less privileged than us. Humanity somewhere still exists in all of us and as a result when we are going in a car and we see someone on the road begging or selling something in scorching heat so that they can at least provide a one-time meal to their family, we feel bad.

When we see someone in a helpless condition where they are begging us to save their mother or child from dying because they can't, we feel bad. When someone is born without parents and has no one to look after them, we feel bad. When someone is born without hands or legs or is mentally disturbed and has to live their whole life like that, we naturally feel bad looking at them. We might not be in their shoes and we can't even imagine living like that, in such situations, yet we feel bad for them.

We all feel bad for them but that feeling goes as fast as it comes and we move on with our lives. We believe that they were destined to live like that but what if we were destined to help them and make their life better? We never try to think of a million ways in which we can help a person. We don't always have to give them money, we can give them food, shelter, our clothes, our care and whatever else possible for us.

By doing this we are not only making them happy but also ourselves happy with the smile we bring on their faces and with the blessings they give us. We don't have to do a lot to make someone else's life better because even our small efforts count. They don't expect a lot from us - just a little humanity and care. In life it doesn't matter how much we have, what matters is how much we give, because the more we give the more we get back in return and the best smile is that which we see on someone else's face because of us. That is real happiness.

7. Accept and let go

We all want to be in a happy, carefree state where we can do whatever we want. We all want to be happy from within all the time, however, we cannot always be that way. There are so many things that hold us back. There are so many things we give so much control and importance in our life. There are so many things we hold onto when we should let go already. There are so many bad things we remember while we so easily forget all the good that a person has done for us.

In reality, we choose to hold onto the bad more than the good. Those situations may not need that reaction or that much amount of importance but nevertheless we give it. We let small things affect us so much. We don't forgive, forget or let go. We keep replaying bad instances and situations in our head and by holding onto those bad memories, we not only hurt our self, but we also hurt someone else as a result of it.

We don't realise the amount of pain we cause just by holding onto the past. Betrayal, heartbreak, backstabbing, disappointments, politics, deceiving - we all have felt these things at some point or other in our life and it had the biggest impact on us, because most of the time, it came from the closest people. Yet life didn't stop, did it? We got stronger, we survived, we learned to come in terms with reality, we learnt our lessons and moved on.

That's how, we as human beings, learn to survive. However, we need to learn to wear our pain like a symbol of our strength and come in terms with reality because no matter how much we obsess over our past and how we could have done things differently, the truth is, we can't now. It is what it is and all we can do is accept and let go. If we still hold onto the past, we continuously keep choosing to ruin our present as well as our future. So, let's allow ourselves to grow and accept the fact that whatever happens in our life, happens for the best.

As it is, we don't have a lot of control over our life. We can't change our past or see our future. All we have is now, this moment; so let's live it fully because that is another thing we are never getting back. It is easy to live a life full of regrets, it is very easy to hold onto our past forever but what is difficult is, learning something from it and moving on and being grateful for all the bad things that happened to us because they got us here, they made us who we are today.

Just think about it; even the worst situation that has happened to us could've got much worse and yet it didn't. So, we still have so much to be grateful and happy about, we just don't see it yet. A lot of people are born with a horrible past, a lot of people live through it. There is only one way of truly overcoming it. Forgive, forget, accept the past, learn from our mistakes, be grateful that things aren't as bad as they could be, let go, stay happy and embrace every good thing that is coming to us with open arms because we truly deserve it.

8. Reconnect with nature

The most beautiful things are often the ones we don't pay attention to. Their beauty can be seen but few know their value and stop to admire it. One such thing is our mother nature. We see her everywhere we go; as a matter of fact we are surrounded by her miracles, but we hardly stop and admire them. We travel hours together to watch a beautiful sunset, we climb an entire mountain to see its view from the top and we continue to travel thousands of kilometres in search of something that is always around us.

Nature. And yet we don't value it enough. We cut thousands of trees every day, we pollute lakes and rivers, we omit so many harmful gases in the environment and we continue to do things that ruin something that has been so thoughtfully and beautifully gifted to us. However, we keep taking steps to destroy the environment in the name of growth and industrialization. We never stop to wonder why we are doing all this and at what cost.

We move around in a busy world trying to find our self, the meaning of our life and peace and happiness and we often find ourselves getting all this from the warmth of nature. Think about it - nothing can be compared to the cool breeze and peaceful sleep we get when we sleep under a big tree or the smile on our face when we watch a beautiful sunset or when we step out to enjoy and dance in the rain.

Nature always finds a way to heal and teach us so many valuable lessons with such deep meanings. Everything around us has the power to make us happy and teach us something meaningful but all we need to really do, is stop for a moment and recognize its beauty. Let it empower us and our minds in so many beautiful ways.

Not everyone needs to go to the Himalayas to find themselves and their peace of mind.

If we really want to be happy then we must leave our home and take a walk in nature, go cycling or trekking or take a trip right in the midst of the wild and realize how easy it really is, to survive and be happy. It takes nothing, all we really have to do is connect with nature and let it guide us. There is no better way of being happy on an eventual permanent basis. Nature is the best medicine we can get.

9. Focus on what is going right in our life

We all go through problems and stress on a frequent basis in our life and they always seem to have a significant impact on us. The worst thing is that we stay stuck on it and constantly worry and dwell on it. Our problems find a way of staying in our mind and keep us wondering. Small things can ruin our mood in minutes. We can be happy the whole day and one small incident might ruin our entire mind frame and our happy-go-lucky attitude.

This happens to everyone and trust me when I tell you, it will continue to happen; we only have to find a way to deal with it. We have to stop giving so much power to the things, people and surroundings around us. We have to take control of our life and how we deal with it because at the end of the day we are the ones who are most affected by it. So, we need to pay more attention to what affects us, how much, what and who we let in.

If we don't focus on these things, they are bound to have a big impact on us and affect us. The cause of most of our misery comes from the fact that we often focus on the wrong things in life. We get so involved with what is going wrong with us that we fail to see things that are already working for us. For example, on a scale of one to ten, if nine things are working in our favour, and we decide to focus on the one thing that's going wrong, then we will never be happy.

We need to stop giving so much importance to our problems because no matter how big they may seem at present, they are not going to last. Every time we find our self-unhappy or being pulled back by something, all we need to do is ask our self if this is going to matter after five years and if not then just let it be, let go and stay happy. This is not hard once we start realising the importance of our peace of mind and our happiness.

All we need to do is change our focus from wrong things or situations to right ones, from negative to positive, from problems to solutions and it will result in a transformation of our life, our thinking and of our mindset. Practising gratitude also helps us to focus on the right things in life and stay happy. In order to stay happy, we have to free our mind from all negative thoughts and energies and focus on self-growth. After all we owe our self every bit of happiness we can get.

D. Let out the negative

1. Don't dwell on setbacks or failure

In life, things don't always happen our way. Nor do things go the way we intended them to. In the final moment there is always something that changes or comes in between like a problem or a hindrance. No matter how perfectly we plan something with all the details and precisions, in the final moment the situation changes and an alternative course of action has to be taken. This is because of the dependencies on the external environment.

When we are so dependent on the external environment for success, changes in them tend to have a huge impact on our business. Therefore, it is very important for us to do market research before we start any business, in order to understand the needs and demands of the consumers and stay better prepared. However, no amount of research can guarantee success. At the end of the day, we have to adapt to the changing environment and bounce back from failures and setbacks.

When we live in such an uncertain, ever-changing environment, we are more open to risks and setbacks and as a result it is more challenging to succeed and achieve our goals. However, we should never stop trying, especially in our bad times because those are the times that test our strength and determination the most. The people who are successful aren't those who never failed. They are those people who never stopped trying regardless of their failure.

Everyone goes through a bad time at some point of time or other. No business ever runs on the same scale, there are always ups and downs. In bad times we need to face them head on, show strength, determination, accept things and move on because at the end of the day our failures don't define us, our success does and the people who survive in this tough competitive market are the ones who never gave up or stopped believing in themselves even for a day.

Therefore, we need to keep ourselves positively motivated at all times. We need to be our strongest believer and stop letting our setback or failure define us because we are so much more than that. People who are happy or succeed in life aren't the ones who don't fall; as a matter of fact, they fall the most but their failure does not scare them. So, we need to believe in our self, our potential and worth and never ever give up or stop trying because until we don't give up, no one can make us lose and till the time we stay strong and positive, no one can make us unhappy.

2. Leave ego behind

Maintaining our relations or friendships in life is not always easy. As years go by, it becomes a task, to constantly find time to talk to each other, meet, be involved in each other's lives and help each other through tough times. Most people cannot do so much and as a result we drift away. We lose a lot of people in this process. However, the people who truly love us and overcome all this to stay with us, we find a way of pushing them away too through fights, anger and our big fat ego.

It is sad really that we let our ego ruin our friendships with people. Most people confuse ego with self-respect. They think the bigger the ego, the more the self-respect. But, it's quite the opposite. Our ego and self-respect are two very different things. Our self-respect comes out of our love for our self while ego comes into picture when we start being too sensitive about things. Now, I am not saying that we shouldn't have ego. We are proud beings so when someone insults us, ego naturally comes in place.

However, anything to a limit is good in our life, be it ego or self-respect. But when anything gets excessive it causes a problem. For instance, when someone continuously feeds their ego and gets too egoistic with time, a slight hit in their ego and they get offended in no time. They also get really angry and might even be rude to everyone around them as a result of that. Egoistic people are also extremely sensitive. We might be joking around them but we never know when they will take it on their ego and get upset about it.

It is extremely difficult to be around such people because they have constant mood swings and are angry most of the time. Most people don't even understand why they are so angry and why they have to take everything so personally; sometimes nor do they but that is how they become. Imagine, if we spend half our life in anger and the other half feeling bad about how we acted out because of the anger, is there really any space for happiness or anything good in our life?

We have to learn to control our emotions and not let them overpower us. We have to accept the fact that we have become egoistic and then consciously find ways of reducing it. In order to live a happier life, we have to be able to control our anger and how we respond to it. Also, we need to get our priorities straight. We need to respect the people around us. If we even have a fight with them, we need to put our ego away and say sorry. We don't become the smaller person by doing that, but in fact, the greater one. In the end, we have to make a choice between an egoistic life and a happier one because both cannot co-exist.

3. We are never ready like we want to be

In life, we always use excuses as a reason to not do real work. This can be said in terms of our workout, creativity, learning something new, following our dreams or completing our goals. We have trained our minds to be lazy and come up with excuses. For instance, if we decide to diet from today onwards but we come across our favourite dish or something we really like, we instantly think that today I will cheat on my diet but from tomorrow I will start again.

No matter how ready or firm we are, there is always a small thought inside our head that will stop us and tell us we can do this tomorrow, let's just rest for now, and funnily enough we listen to this voice almost always because all we need is an excuse to delay things. That's how lazy we are as human beings. We want to do so much in life, we want to achieve so much, but sadly we don't even work half as much as we should for that.

We always wait for the perfect moment. We wait for everything to be as we expect it to be, but the truth is there will always be something which could cause a hindrance or problem, and our perception of a perfect moment is a myth not a reality. It is something we tell ourselves to not do something and feel better about it and most of the time it works because we think we have so much time to do anything that a little delay won't be a problem.

But time is the one thing that none of us have. A moment once gone never comes back. All we have is now. This moment, this time. So, work now, do things now, learn now because we have no idea what tomorrow might bring! So, make the most out of this moment because we are never going to be ready like we want to be but we have to start somewhere. We have to stop waiting for the perfect moment and take steps in the right direction.

This will not only make us more proactive but it will also make us happier. Just imagine if we did everything we always wanted to do. How excited and happier would we be because we would be following our heart and living our best potential! This will also have a huge impact on our confidence and overall personality. We would be living not only the best present but also work towards the best future. All we have to do for a happier life is stop delaying things, live today fully and then think about tomorrow.

4. Don't spend time or energy on resentment of other people's success

We live in a world where we are surrounded by social media and its influence can be seen in each and every part of our life. Nowadays, we are more interested in increasing our followers than having real friends, we are more interested in smiling and posing for pictures than being in that moment and having fun, we are more interested in going to good places and showing our superiority to others than actually living a good life and we are more interested to live a reel life rather than living a real one.

We are all misguided and unknowingly dragged in a race to do something just because it is trending or to go somewhere because everyone is going or eating something just because everyone is eating. This negative influence happens to everyone at one or the other point of time in their life. We are all surrounded by social media, so much so that we have all got inferiority . We are trying to do things to show we are having fun, living a great life, spending so much money when the reality is something else.

For this exact reason, we need to stop spending so much of our time in resentment of other people's success because everything that we see on social media may not necessarily be true. We don't really know what happened there or their reality. So, there is no point in sinking in grief thinking someone is having a better life than us because we are fine the way we are and life is not a race. Moreover, success is a very personal thing and everyone achieves it at their own time.

There is no right time or age for that. Someone may be very successful when they are 25 but shut down their business due to major losses at 40 and on the other hand, we may start our business at 35 but it may successfully run our whole life. We never know what life has in store for us. Everyone does things in their own time and when they are ready, so it's okay if all our friends have jobs and are successful but we are nowhere right now. Someday we will reach somewhere as well.

Our comparison is only with our self because we only live our story. So, there is absolutely no point in resenting someone else's success because that only makes us bitter and sad. Instead, let's focus on our life and our journey and be happy with whatever we have achieved so far even if it's less. All we need to do is just believe in our self, keep working hard, keep following our dreams and know that we will one day reach where we are destined to be. Always remember, don't be sad because of someone else, instead be happy for yourself. It's much more worth it.

5. Fear

Fear, I believe, is the strongest four-letter word because it has a grasp on not only our mind, but our body, our brain, our heart, everything. It has a way of controlling us and preventing us from doing certain things. I don't think there is even one person alive on this earth who is not fearful of something even if he is the richest, smartest or the most intelligent man in the room. Everyone is scared of something and everyone has their reasons for it but fear is an emotion which is present in each and every creature that lives on this earth.

The most basic fear is that of death. Everyone wants to survive and our will to survive and keep moving on despite everything that is going on with us, helps us to stay alive. But our life has its own ups and downs like our heartbeat and we wish for stability in our life. For everything to just pause and for us to be happy forever. But, in the moment our life and heartbeat become a straight line it's game over for us. As a result, we scar not only our self but also the people who are close to us.

We fear death so much, not only for our self but also for people who are closest to us, that if anything happens to them it becomes extremely difficult for us to move on and be happy. We give so much power to our fear that it becomes our biggest weakness and ends up becoming one of the biggest hindrances of our life. For example, if someone is scared of water and they are thrown into the swimming pool, the fear of water will not only take over their mind, but their entire body and they may even become numb.

Even if they are rescued, they would have to live with that incident every time they see a pool or close their eyes and it could be their biggest nightmare. That is how powerful fear is and no one can save us from it but our self. In order to move on with our life and live a happy life, we have to face our fear. Bit by bit we have to reduce the effect it has on us because the more we are scared of it, the more powerful our fear becomes. It is like a demon living inside of us that has the power to destroy us and no one else can do anything about it.

We have to save our self, we have to be stronger, we have to stop being scared and face our fear head on because at the end of the day it is nothing but a mind block. A fear that we have developed in ourselves. A reaction that we have developed by thinking we are scared of this. So, the only way of dealing with it is to face our fear and survive. Once we know we can survive in the face of fear, we would no longer be scared of it. As a result, it would have no control over us and we would move on to live a much happier life. In this fight between our fear and us, let's make sure we win always and stay happy.

6. Don't regret

Our mind is a beautiful collection of so many things, moments and memories. We may not remember each and every one of them but we always remember those memories that are very close to our heart and are very special to us. These are the memories that our mind stores and we remember them even after years together. Sometimes when we think about them, we laugh, sometimes we cry,

sometimes we just look back at a much simpler time and think how much we have changed along with the things around us.

To have something to hold onto and remember, is a beautiful thing. However, not everything we hold onto is worth remembering. Sometimes our mind stocks even the worst things that happened to us. Those things which sadden us or bring us down. Many times we keep remembering the mistakes we made in the past and while we might have moved on now, that memory still brings along with it a certain amount of sadness and emptiness with us wishing things would have happened differently.

We all go through this at some point of time, while some might call it self-reflection, some call it regret. But what really happens when we regret things? We feel low, we feel sad, we feel disheartened in the memory of what happened. We feel horrible for our words or actions and we think of a thousand ways in which we could have dealt differently with the situation and maybe we could have that time. But the reality is, now in this moment when we think about it, can we change anything?

We need to ask our self this question again and again until we know for sure that we cannot do anything about it now and if we really cannot do anything about it now then we should stop thinking about it and hurting our self. There is not much achieved by regret other than pain. Everyone keeps making mistakes in their life, it is a part of growing up. Until we don't make mistakes, we don't learn.

If we really feel bad about the mistakes we have made, then we must make amends, learn from our mistakes and not repeat them again.

Regret and guilt do not make that or any future situation any better. We will keep making mistakes because we are human beings and that is what we are meant to do but we cannot keep feeling guilty about all the mistakes we make because then we will be stuck in our past. We will never be able to move ahead in life and be happy. So, if we really want to be happy all we need to do is accept our mistake, make amends and move on to a happier life that awaits us.

7. Stop trying to be perfect

Our childhood builds a foundation for the rest of our life. What we are taught in our childhood, our values and virtues, they stay with us always. We follow them sometimes, sometimes we don't, but they always help us to differentiate between right and wrong. It also tends to have a major impact on the habits and the discipline that we follow throughout our life like brushing our teeth before going to bed, keeping our things in place, washing our hands before eating food. These are things that we have been practising since our childhood.

Every parent wants their kid to be the best and to shine out among the crowd. For this exact reason, they pressurize them to do everything and be perfect in it. They push us to excel in sports, get better marks, make us join so many classes and the list goes on and on. For most people, getting a 'well-done *beta*' from their parents is not easy. Due to this reason they keep working hard their entire life to win their appreciation.

They keep striving to be perfect for them and before they realise it, it becomes a habit to be perfect at everything. However, perfection can never be attained. Perfection is nothing but a myth. It's as good as chasing a ghost when we can never catch it. It's a very tiring process to be perfect always and to be the best in everything because no matter how much we do, it never seems to be enough. The process of chasing perfection is never-ending. People who chase perfection require everything to work well, be perfect and go as planned.

But does life always work according to our plan? It always gifts us surprises and improvisations have to be made from our end. However, if things don't go our way, we start being very unhappy with it because people who believe in being perfect at all times are control freaks. They don't like changes; they overthink and analyse themselves and the things around them at every step. They are very harsh on themselves and they constantly put pressure on themselves to be better.

It becomes extremely hard for such people to love themselves, take appreciations well or praise themselves when they do something good and this often reflects on all their relationships. But we need to remember at the end of the day that no matter how much we try, we are going to make mistakes. We will never be perfect enough because as human beings there is always so much scope for growth, so we need to stop putting so much pressure on our self and cut our self some slack. No matter how much we try we cannot control everything. So, let things flow the way they have to and be happy with what we have because at the end of the day nothing is going to be perfect and that's okay because it's not about being perfect, it's about being right.

8. Mindset

Our life is a collection of our thoughts. Everything we think reciprocates in reality in some form or another. For this exact reason, we have to be very careful with what we think because that is what we attract in our life. Our thoughts also form our mindset and the way we start seeing things. A same piece of work if someone thinks is easy, they will do it faster in less time and if someone thinks is hard, they will do it slower taking more time. So, it's all about what we tell our mind or how and by whom we let it get influenced.

For instance, we start liking certain colours, bands, singers or actors simply because our friends or the people around us like it. That is why it is very important for us to choose our close circle wisely because they have the biggest impact on us before we even realise it. Our mind is so innocent that it easily gets influenced positively and negatively by the people around us. Our mind does not actually have a brain of its own and sadly it cannot differentiate between right and wrong.

It is like a robot that we programme. It only feeds any data we give it by thoughts and feelings and it stores it. This data when processed comes out in terms of words and actions. So, it is extremely important that we think right because based on that, we start feeling that way about things, then a mindset gets formed and we start acting accordingly. A mindset is nothing but a collection of thoughts and feelings regarding any particular thing. Since, our thoughts and feelings towards things keep changing as we meet new people, our mindset also keeps changing as we grow.

This is why we loved Barbies or cars when we were kids and now, we don't because the way we started feeling about them changed as we grew. Similarly, a lot of people hate alcohol initially but with time they develop a taste for it and love it because how they felt about it changed and with that their mindset towards it also changed. Whenever we have a very strong mindset about something it becomes our perception and that is how we start seeing things.

Due to this reason it is extremely important for us to have a positive mindset and see the best in everything. We also need to think positive, feel good and have a developed mindset for us to be happy and to deal with things in a better way. Therefore, we have to be very careful with what we think and monitor our thoughts always. If any negative thought comes our way, we can instantly change it to positive. At the end of the day it's all about having a happy and positive mind. Remember, it always starts with a thought so make sure it is good and life-changing.

9. Don't jump to conclusions

We all live in a world where it is very normal for people to have fights,

disagreements, misunderstandings etc. It is part of every relationship that we have

and is important to us in our life. Some think it is healthy to have fights

every once in a while, it makes the bond stronger. It also makes us realise where we are going wrong and gives us time for self-evaluation. Any relationship is a mixture of a lot of emotions. Where there is love, there has to be anger, where there is happiness, there has to be sadness and where there is excitement, there has to be disappointment.

Life is about finding the perfect balance in everything we do and feel. However

when the balance is not maintained, there is always a problem. When there is one

person in a relationship who loves more or gives more, it tends to cause problems between those two people. But what really destroys a relationship is when those two people continuously misunderstand each other, blame each other, fight over everything instead of talking things out. It is a long way of suppressed emotions and toxicity. But somewhere it all starts from miscommunications and when they both jump to conclusions.

Now, jumping to conclusions over everything is very normal to us as human beings, because we have a habit of overthinking and analysing everything. We have to believe that we are right always and we know everything. However, what we see is what we think we know and what we hear is what is true for us. But there is so much we don't know and obviously miss out on. It is the fear of the unknown that forces us to jump to conclusions with the information we have.

So, when we don't know exactly what happened or why that person did what he did, it is very wrong on our part to directly jump to conclusions, because by doing this, we are not only misunderstanding the other person but making our own versions of the story and being upset over it. Also, whatever incomplete information we grasp, we talk about it to our friends and close ones and directly or indirectly start a rumour about something.

That's why it is always advisable to clear things out when we are in a doubt about it. Sit with that person, talk, tell them how we feel in a very nice, comfortable manner. This not only helps to avoid a fight but also helps both the people in the discussion maintain good relations for a lifetime. This is any day better than keeping things in our mind where they will keep troubling us and come out in a very inappropriate way. Avoid jumping to conclusions, continue communication and stay happy. It is the secret to maintaining a happy relationship.

E. Work on yourself

1. Connect with something you love

As kids we had so many dreams and such great imagination. We could build castles and become superheroes in our mind. We were extremely energetic and creative and Lord knows nothing could tie us down. We would continuously run from this end to that end, play all day, fall, get up and start running again. Nothing and nobody could stop us at that time. So, what exactly happened when we grew up? Except having a bigger body, looks to die for and more intelligence, what really changed in us?

Have we ever just stopped and wondered where all that energy, enthusiasm, willpower and happiness went? After all these years, these are the questions whose answers we still don't have. Life was so much easier as a kid. We didn't have to think so much, we could just eat and sleep all the time and everything was good. As kids we always wanted to be some amazing personality like a doctor, astronaut or a soldier but, how many of us grew up to live that dream? Sadly, a very few.

Even now there are so many things we want do but they just stay in our mind.

We never actually take the efforts to do the things we love. Things that we always wanted to do or learn, like cooking, speaking a new language, dancing and so on. The reason it was easier to be happier when we were kids is because we just did what we loved, we never thought so much and that's exactly what we need to do now. We need to be that happy kid again and connect with something we love. We need to find time for things that are truly important to us.

Regardless of how busy we are with our jobs, our friends, roaming around the whole day or passing time on the phone, in our busy lives we need to find time for ourselves. Not much, maybe just an hour everyday where we just do things to make ourselves happy. Just 'me time'. For this, we can either connect with things we love or discover things that make us happy.

There is a whole list of things that we always wanted to do that we haven't done yet, another list of things that we have never even tried and a completely different list of things that we will end up doing when we start these two and the sooner we start this list the more fun and exciting life will get. Discovering our self, our happiness and the meaning of our life is the biggest job any of us can have. So, start now because there is no better time like today. After all, we owe the kid within us every bit of happiness we can provide.

2. Create a morning routine

Imagine waking up to a pink sky, snow-covered mountains, a waterfall and flowers everywhere our eyes can find. What beautiful scenery this is. It is something which can blow our mind and waking up to this will naturally bring a big smile on our face. Now imagine, when someone wakes us up by throwing on us a glass of cold water or switching off the fan or taking off our blanket or hitting us. How irritated do we feel when this happens? We just want to kill the person who does this. As a result, this irritation is likely to stay with us the whole day.

Someone has very smartly said how we start our day has a huge impact on how our entire day goes. If we start our day on a good note with a smile, a lot of dreams in our eyes and a positive attitude, we are more likely to have a great day filled with joy. Things will go our way and one positive start can lead to our entire day going well. On the other hand, when our day starts with shouting at someone or cussing, we are more likely to have a bad day ahead. Consequently, more bad things will follow us the whole day.

The universe works very precisely and it picks up every signal that we send it.

According to the law of attraction, everything we send out finds a way of coming back to us. Every thought that we have, has a frequency whether it is positive or negative. The frequency we are on, is what we attract in our life. So, even if we start our day on the wrong foot with a lot of negative thoughts in our mind, we can change those negative thoughts to positive ones and reassure our self that we are happy and we are going to have a great day ahead. This will help us attract goodness and stay happy always.

But how can we make sure our mornings start on a good note always? Have a morning routine. Wake up early in the morning, meditate, go out for a run or exercise. Eat good healthy food and have lots of fruits in the morning. This is very good for digestion and keeps our mind sharp and helps us plan our entire day. When we start our day on such a positive and high energy note we are more likely to feel good and energetic the whole day. Also, our mind is most fresh when we wake up.

So, this is also a very good time to study because we grasp a lot in a short period of time or to start working because we are likely to work more, feel motivated and finish our work by noon or think up new creative ideas because our mind is not tired in the morning so it works more. Morning as we now know is the most important part of our day. Yet as most of us spend it by sleeping and lazing around, all the successful people use this time of the day to do most of their work. So, get up and start working to a much happier morning and thus a much happier life ahead. We cannot decide how our day ends but we can always decide how it starts.

3. Share your gifts and talents with the world

As kids we were made to join so many classes and learn so many different things like dancing, skating, drawing and so on. That time we didn't understand much as to why we had to learn so many things but we never questioned it. Everything we were taught, we learned in a proper manner and as we grew, it became easier for us to realise the things that we are actually good at. This helped us to pursue those hobbies and be the best at them.

However, everyone is good at different things because God has made us all differently. There is something that differentiates us from each other. It may be our looks, our personality, our job or our hobbies. But, every person no matter how smart or dumb, they are gifted with a special talent. This is the one thing that defines us and gives a meaning to our life. While some of us already know this special talent of ours, others spend a lifetime finding it.

But when we find it, a lot of us just let it go away. We become so busy with life that most of us don't get time to work on this gift or talent of ours. Instead of pursuing this talent, we run behind money and get caught up in the corporate world and our entire life goes by like that. But think about it, if Sachin Tendulkar would have been a lawyer would we have known him or loved him so much? Or if Roger Federer would have worked as an accountant how much would the world have missed out on!

When we actually think about it, we realise that these people are best at what they do simply because they found their talent and followed their heart. They also believed in themselves and chased their dreams. That is why they are so successful and happy in life right now. Simply, because they didn't let their talent go to waste and they actually worked towards it. Similarly, we all need to share our gifts and talents with the world. We need to believe in our self. We need to stop being so scared of failure, follow our heart and chase after our dreams.

After all, what we have is special, unique and beautiful. Not everyone has the same gift. So, instead of running behind money or happiness let us run behind the thing that we are best at and let money and happiness follow. It may have been a long time since we last practised but with hard work and perseverance, anything can be achieved. It's never too late to start. To finally live the life of our dreams which everyone will remember. We owe this to our self, to the world, to our millions of followers and to those kids who will one day dream to be like us.

4. Set smarter goals

Most of us are stuck in jobs all our life because we are too scared to start something on our own and face the uncertainties the outside world has to offer. We live in fear of flying solo, taking risks and failing. That is why we work under someone else, follow the company guidelines and take a fixed amount of money home. However, even if we do get the courage to do something on our own someday, we expect it to be an instant hit right from the start.

We naturally feel like that because we invest so much of our time, money and effort in starting a business of our own, that we need it to run well to cover our expenses. However, every business runs at its own course and it normally takes time for the business to establish itself. It takes time for the product to be known, for us to build a brand image, for us to rise among the competition, to gain customers and increase their satisfaction with the product or brand.

It takes many years for us to just cover our expenses and then start winning profits. It is a long tedious process, where we live in such an ever-changing business environment that success is never guaranteed. When we live in such an uncertain business environment, we have to set smarter goals and we have to stop letting our losses and the constant business ups and downs make us so unhappy. We have to stay strong to face things. When we set our goals, the bar can neither be too high nor too low.

If our goals are too high, it would become extremely difficult for us to achieve them. Having such unrealistic goals demotivates the employees and puts everyone under a lot of pressure. Even then, we wouldn't be happy because our goals will not be achieved and even if we have done more than before, it wouldn't seem enough. However, if our goals are too low, it would become extremely easy for us to achieve them and it wouldn't push us to achieve our potential. Also, it wouldn't give us the feeling of satisfaction or joy over having achieved something.

Our goals therefore, should be such that they are realistic but attainable. We must always think rationally before setting our goals because when we set smarter goals, we are more likely to achieve them and stay happy. We should discuss our goals with the employees and help them be a part of the decision-making process. This will motivate them to work harder towards the completion of the goal. Also, we must set attainable goals every day to ensure that we are on the right track and thus enjoy conquering every little goal and step in life. Happiness after all, is not always about the big things, but it is about enjoying even the small steps that we take in our life.

5. Manage time effectively

For most people, 2020 has been the worst year. It has been a year of suffering and pain. While the world economy has collapsed, most countries are doing what they can to tackle Coronavirus. Everyone is in a state of shock due to its massive outreach. While the number of cases kept increasing each day, so many innocent people died around the world. The government therefore, initiated a lockdown and pledged people to stay home and stay safe.

However, in this lockdown, most people just wasted their time instead of doing something productive. Everyone either binge-watched movies and series or played PUBG the whole day or funnily enough done both. People just found a way to pass their time until the phase went away and even after Corona gets over most people would still be wasting all their time doing something unimportant. There are a very few people who have seen this as an opportunity, managed their time well and made the most out of it.

This is the biggest problem with most of us. We don't know how to manage our time well. Time is the biggest resource we are all equally gifted with but how many of us make the best utilisation of our given time? We always take time for granted until it is the one thing that we do not have anymore. For instance, we don't study throughout the year and panic when exams come. Then, we make a timetable that we never follow properly because of our bad time management skills and end up studying one night before the exam.

When we have something, we take it casually and we realise its importance only when it's gone. Our inefficient time management has a very negative impact on the relationships we have. Especially, if we cannot maintain the balance between our family, friends, work and personal life. Problems start emerging in each area of our life and it becomes very difficult to tackle. Also, we all have limited time on this earth so it is very important that we make the best use of it and make a lot of memories with our friends and family while we can, otherwise we will only be left with regrets in life.

Therefore, managing our time well is extremely important for us to gain maximum productivity and to achieve our goals and live a life of happiness. So, start making time tables and start following them, have weekly reminders and allocate time to each thing that is done every day. So, we can do everything we enjoy while we make the most out of it. Start realising where we waste our time and slowly start reducing that. We all have 24 hours in a day regardless of the fact if we are rich or poor. How we utilise this time is what makes all the difference in the world. People who are successful value and respect their time and that's what makes them who they are. It's about time we start doing the same.

6. Dreams

Dreams are the one thing that we watch with our eyes open as well as our eyes closed. While some daydream because they are bored, some dream even with their eyes closed. Our dreams be it good or bad, is something that our mind always remembers. Our dreams are the things that we want to achieve in our life and they push us to move forward and keep working hard. If we didn't have any dreams or goals in life, our life would hardly have any meaning. It is our dreams which give meaning to our life and make it beautiful.

However, in order to achieve our dreams, we must always follow our heart because our heart always guides us in the right direction. Our heart always knows best and helps us take the correct decisions with the help of our instincts. So, in order to follow our dreams, we need to follow our heart and in order to follow our heart we must trust our instincts. Now, we all dream for a better future but how many of us take the efforts it takes to get there? Having dreams or goals in life is not enough. Unless it is backed by hard work and perseverance, it has no meaning. Until then, it is just a thought in our head.

When we see a dream or set a goal in life, we need to make sure that it is big enough to motivate us and make us get up from sleep to work towards it. If Virat Kohli would have settled with playing cricket for just the state or on a national level, he would not have been the captain of the Indian cricket team. Similarly, if Mukesh Ambani would have settled with just earning good money for his family, he would not be the richest man in India today. The similarity among all the people who are successful today is that their dreams were big always and they dreamed about being Number One.

So, they kept working hard and never settled with just doing good. They continuously pushed themselves to be their best and give their best. Completing all our goals and dreams in life is one of the biggest joys we can achieve. The journey though might be tough but, it is always worth remembering. Achieving a certain place in life is hard but what is even harder, is maintaining it. The easier it is to climb up, the harder it becomes to stay there. It takes a continuous amount of hard work and determination to keep moving ahead in life.

But, in life we only remember the people who followed their dreams and kept working hard to reach where they are today. Having dreams is not a privilege. Poor people think that they don't have any right to have any dreams because their dreams never get fulfilled. However, most of the people who are successful today were once poor with a desire to make it big. The difference between them and all of us is that they didn't use excuses to not achieve something, instead they found solutions. Nothing is impossible in life when we keep working hard and keep dreaming, because the closer we are to our dreams, the closer we always will be to our happiness.

7. Stop being dependent on others

We spend most of our life being dependent on others to provide us the things that we want. Like for example, as kids we naturally depend on our parents to pay for our school and buy us what we want, which is okay then, because we are unable to earn ourselves at that time and we are our parents' responsibility. But the habit of being dependent on others for the things that we want has always been there in us and is still prevalent in us whether we agree to this or not. One such thing for which we are mainly dependent on others is our happiness.

We always expect others to make us happy by saying or doing stuff that makes us happy and we always want those things or situations to occur around us which will make us happy. But life does not work like that and nor do the people around us. So, we cannot put conditions on our happiness. Like for example, if we are wearing a pretty dress, we will wait for someone to compliment us in order for us to be happy, when we work hard and achieve something, we always want everyone to appreciate us and we always want everyone to think and say good things about us. But why does our happiness come with so many conditions?

When we depend on others to make us happy, we are more likely to be disappointed because how someone else thinks or what they say or how they behave is never in our control. People do as they like and they hardly stop to think about the impact it has on us. Everybody is just living their life and doing things which make them happy. Hence, having so many expectations from others will naturally make us disappointed and sad. We cannot expect others to do as much we do for them or have the same understanding level that we have because that is practically impossible.

We are responsible for our own actions and we must stay happy in giving rather than getting. We need to understand that no one in this whole wide world can make us happy if we do not want to be happy. Happiness is something which should come from within. It is something inside us and it is only we who can give it to our self. So, let us stay happy on our own and stop giving others the power to decide whether they can make us happy or not because being dependent on others for our happiness is a total waste of time as it will always result in disappointment. Letting others decide our happiness will lead us to live a life of unhappiness.

If we truly want to live a life of happiness, let us be our own source of happiness and decide to be happy always. For this, we need to stop letting what others say or do have such a big impact on us. If someone says something negative about us, we need to stop giving that thing the power to affect us. We need to know our self and our strengths very well and stop feeling like we owe anyone in this world an explanation because honestly, we are better than that and we are stronger than that. And at the end of the day, we are all we've got, so we have to look after ourselves and keep our best interests at heart. No one knows us better than we do and that is exactly why no one can make us as happy as we can make ourselves.

8. Stay active don't retire

Imagine what would happen if we just sit at home for five months or more with absolutely no workout and all we do is sit, eat, work, watch movies and sleep. Wouldn't we become like an inflated balloon? With an excessive five or ten kgs at a minimum to lose? Just thinking about it brings us under so much pressure. It is difficult for us to even imagine our self like that. All chubby and cute but with none of our clothes fitting us. What a nightmare that would be! We cannot even bear the thought of it and imagine if that became our reality.

Every time we looked in the mirror instead of seeing a beautiful girl or a handsome guy we once were, all we see is someone with imperfections. Now, imagine the reaction of all our friends and relatives when they see us. It would be so embarrassing to hear them talk and laugh at us right on our face. We would wish we could just disappear somewhere and this is what always happens with an overweight person. They are always in guilt of eating outside, they feel ashamed every time they see themselves in the mirror and they are under constant stress to lose weight.

Because of the lockdown initiated, this is exactly what has happened. Almost everyone has gained weight just sitting at home. Gaining weight is easy, it hardly takes any effort, but losing weight becomes a task. We can gain a lot of weight in a month but it might take us three months to lose that weight. Being overweight is not the only problem, being underweight is also a big problem. Therefore, it is extremely necessary for us to keep working out every day and not just sit at home and sulk.

This not only helps us to keep our calories in check but also helps us to stay fit. Someone who works out everyday is more likely to feel alive, they are more energetic and their brain works at a much faster speed. If we workout every day we wouldn't have to be in the pressure of losing or gaining weight because we would be so maintained. Also, we could wear whatever we liked without thinking twice. Most girls would know what a blessing that is and how happy that could make us. Some people have amazing metabolism and no matter what they eat, they never gain weight.

Even then, it is essential for everyone to workout regardless of the fact they are underweight, overweight or the perfect weight. Working out helps us to increase our metabolism and helps our mind stay fresh all the time. It helps us stay strong and work on all our major muscles. With workout, it is very important for us to follow a healthy diet. Workout helps in 30% of our losing weight, the other 70% is our diet. So, eat lots of fruits, green vegetables and avoid sweet and oily food totally. We all want to look attractive and good at the end of the day and nothing could bring us more happiness when that happens. But, how many of us are willing to take the efforts it takes to get there?

9. Meditate

People travel thousands of kilometres in search of themselves. Finding our self and our purpose in life has been the biggest challenge we all face. No matter how much we achieve in life, there always comes a time when all of that means nothing. The feelings of emptiness, loneliness, sadness and feeling lost take over our body and mind. Normal things no longer have the power to make us happy and the need to connect with our self and the divine power above grows. A lot of questions start arising in our mind but how do we find the answer to all those questions?

No matter how many questions we have in our mind the answer is always the same; meditation. It is the answer to all our questions, the result of all our prayers and the end result of finding our happiness and peace of mind. People we look up to, like Buddha or Sai Baba, achieved their level of spirituality through meditation. They meditated so much with all of their heart that they could connect with the universe and the divine power above. They could predict the future and perform miracles. They were not necessarily God because God exists in all of us but we made them God with our faith and belief.

However, if we put this same faith and belief in our self, we have no idea what we can achieve in life. There are a lot of ways to be happy and successful in life but there is only one permanent way in which we can find our happiness and peace of mind and that is through meditation. Now, we don't necessarily need to go on a hill top and meditate for hours together like some people did because we can practise meditation in the comforts of our home. In this busy world, where we do not have time for anything or anyone, all we need is just ten minutes for our self.

These ten minutes will be life transforming for us and they will refresh our mind in ways we never imagined. Meditation is best when practiced early in the morning. However, if we are busy at that time, we can practise it in any part of the day, it's not a problem. By practising meditation, we start being calmer and more composed, we feel more connected with our inner being, it helps us to achieve all our goals, makes us feel happy and its benefits are endless. People who meditate are more connected to the Divine. As a result, they generate very positive vibes around them.

They tend to have a positive approach towards life, such people think good, feel good and they attract more positive things towards them. Meditation should be practised by everyone every day. All we have to do is open YouTube, type meditation and follow any one of the meditation videos that are available. If possible, follow the meditation of the seven chakras of life. It is very helpful. Within a few days, we will realise the impact it has on us and how we are already living the happier life we all dreamed of.

10. Self-care

We all love our family and our friends dearly and as a result we always remember to pamper them and take care of them, but in the process, we sometimes forget our self. We give them so much that we forget that we need to be loved and pampered too. For instance, our mother always makes us our favourite dish, gets our favourite things at home, goes to places we like, keeps the house the way everyone likes it, buys us our favourite things and lives the way we like. But, after all these years, does she even remember what she likes?

When was the last time that she even did something for herself? No matter how much we know our mother, I am sure that most of us would not know the answer to this. As a matter of fact, nor would she, because she is selflessly living a life to keep us happy. Her life revolves around us and our needs. But we are busy in our own world. We have our own friends, classes, school, college and even after we come home, we are on our phone all the time, so we hardly have any time for her. So, while she is living a life to make us happy, who is keeping her happy?

Well the answer to this is that she actually needs to be happy by herself. She needs to understand that no one can really make us happy other than our self because our happiness is inside us, so no one can externally give it to us. Also, being happy is our own responsibility so we cannot just get up and put that responsibility on someone else and expect them to act according to how we want because that never works. We need to love our self and take care of our self because at the end of the day we are all we got. We need to indulge in self-care on a more frequent basis and in order to do so, we need to take some time out for our self each day.

How we spend this time is totally on us. We can spend it drinking a cup of coffee and reading a book or connecting with our talents like drawing or painting or we can just sit at home and watch a movie we love. What we do with this time is not important, the fact that we give it to our self is. In order for us to practice self-care on a day-to-day basis we need to be kind to our self, love our self, trust our instincts, follow our dreams, extend our limits, not think or say bad things about our self, forgive our self and pamper our self.

It is very important for each and every one of us to practise self-care every day in order for us to successfully live a happy and healthy life. If we keep living a life for others where we do not give our self any time, we are bound to get frustrated and unhappy with our life. When we give time to our self, we are not only moving closer towards our happiness but also a life of contentment. It is truly said, we can give others what we have ourselves. If we cannot love and care for our self, we probably cannot even do that for anyone else. It all starts with us, so let's be the change we need in our life.

11. Stay strong

We have all been disappointed in our life at some point or another. We have been let down by people, our trust has been broken, our heart has been shattered and we have all felt an immense amount of pain, suffering and failure. We all feel that life is unfair, we are good people and we do not deserve what happened to us. Which is absolutely true. No one deserves anything bad or darkness in their life. Everyone deserves to have a good life and be happy. Regardless, here we are right now, moving on from those bad things as a much stronger and better person.

Everything we thought we could never survive, like we would just die when something happens, when the time came, we drowned, fought for our every breath and made our way back as a survivor because of who we are as humans - we are survivors. Even in our worst times, our will to live is always much more than our will to die and that is exactly what keeps us going on, our need to survive, our need to stay happy and our need to stay strong. It is not easy doing that, especially when we are really hurt and disappointed but we do it every single time.

We fight and overcome every obstacle life throws at us and always come out as much stronger and enhanced because that is who we are; we are warriors and our life is a battlefield. On this battlefield, life keeps throwing us off guard with problems and pain but do we stop and lose the battle because of it? No, we cry, we mourn but we get up, we fight and we survive. And as much as we want to think that we are weak, emotionally driven and a coward, the truth is we are not. Even when we are those things and something really bad happens to us, we might be broken from within, we might be devastated, but we never leave a fight.

At the end of the day we pull our self back together and we stay strong. Whenever something bad happens to us, all we need to do is think how much worse the situation could have got, then be grateful that it is not that bad, feel gratitude towards God for saving us, learn from our mistakes or where we went wrong, because as much as we want to think that we are always right, it is not true. Both the parties are equally responsible or wrong when there is a fight or something goes wrong. Even if we did not do anything wrong, we let something wrong happen to us and that right there is our fault. So yes, learn from our mistakes and move on.

If we keep holding onto our pain or grief, we are only going to invite more misery into our life and lead a very unhappy life. So instead, accepting things and moving on is a much better option because at the end of the day, there are no bad choices or decisions, there is only more learning. And the more we learn, the more we grow. So, keep learning from our mistakes and use them as a stepping stone towards success and a better life as no one is born strong, everyone becomes strong when that is the only choice they have left. So, stay strong always and remember happiness is not only about being happy in the good times but to also cope with the inevitable bad times in order to experience the best possible life overall.

12. Smile more

No matter how good a dress we wear or makeup we put on or even if we wear the best accessories, still, we look best when we are smiling. It is a known fact that people who smile more live a much happier life than the people who don't. Smiling does not only give our muscles some exercise but it is our way of showing our happiness and joy to the world. It is a beautiful feeling to look at something and feel happy. This is why, when we meet someone we love or like spending time with like our friends or family, there is always a smile on our face.

Smiling is not just a polite way of greeting someone but it is our way of showing love to the other person. And the thing about love is, the more love we give, the more we get it back. So, imagine how great our day would be if we spent it with a smile on our face and abundance of love in our heart. Happiness would just follow us then. It would not be something we needed to chase. This is exactly what needs to happen in our life. We need to stop running about happiness and start finding it in everything around us.

In every situation we are in, be it good or bad, if we could just find the strength to face it with a smile on our face and a calm mind, we would naturally be less angry, stress-free and more practical in life. This would also help us see things through, leading us to make better decisions and develop a much better response to things. We are more likely to be happy then. Now, I know every time we smile it does not necessarily mean that we are happy. Smiling and happiness are two completely different things. However, it is a start. Initially when we smile, it might feel forced. But with time, that smile will reach our heart and it will help us to stay happy always.

So, smile every time we see someone we know as this will help us strengthen our bond with them. Smile even when we see strangers as when we smile it does not just make us happy but also the person in front of us because they start smiling too. So, by smiling we really are spreading happiness in the world and also helping others to be happy. It is always nice to be around someone who is full of joy and is always happy. We love their company and their energy. However, this also motivates others to be that way and gives them strength to face their problems the same way, with a smile on their face.

To summarise it all, it doesn't take much to be happy on an everyday eventual basis and to make others happy all we need to do is smile more, laugh more, be crazier, be adventurous and do things we never thought we could and push every boundary by which we have limited our self. When we start being truly happy, we become more positive in life and we start radiating that positivity to the world. We actually start making this world a better place to live in by being happy ourselves. So, what are we waiting for? Smile every moment we live because when we actually look around us, there is so much to be happy for.

THINGS TO AVOID

1. Self-doubt

We doubt ourselves, be it about anything, it shows our lack of confidence in our self. It also shows how scared we are to do certain things. Either ways, it's not good for us. Self-doubt kills happiness, our goals, dreams and all good things coming to us. So, instead of doubting yourself, know that we deserve every good thing coming to us.

2. Toxic addictions

We need to have control over our toxic addictions like drinking, smoking and other things. Every time we are unhappy, we cannot run to doing these. This is not an effective way of dealing with grief and it does not make our problems or pains go away. By engaging in such activities to reduce our pain, we are only adding more misery to our self.

3. Abusive relationships

Being in an abusive relationship takes away every bit of happiness from us. We live in constant fear, pain and feel so powerless. No matter how much we love the other person, that person becomes very toxic for us. It makes us feel horrible and ruins our life. Everyone deserves to be happy and treated well. So, always choose what we deserve and what is best for us.

4. Mediocre friendships

Stop settling for people who do not love us, appreciate us, care for us or value us. People who do not reciprocate the same efforts we make for them are not good for us and they do not help us grow. Such friendship does not help us move ahead in life but only pulls us back. Stop settling for mediocre friendships in life when we deserve better than that.

5. Self-inflicted pain

The worst pain we give our self is through our own thoughts. When we are too harsh on our self, criticize our self or constantly devalue our self we cause a lot of self-inflicted pain. This pain stays with us and affects all our relationships. So, in order to be happy instead of hating our self we need to learn to love our self, be kind to our self and forgive our self for our mistakes.

6. Fear of not being enough

Most of us feel like we are not enough for our friends, family and the people around us. The fear of not being enough is a very strong negative feeling which brings us down and makes us feel like no matter how much we do for them, it is never enough. They don't appreciate or value us. This is exactly why we should do everything for our self. This way we expect less and stay happy more.

7. Living in parts

Most of us live our lives in parts. We enjoy in some parts; we cry in some parts and we stay happy in some parts. However, we should never live our life in parts or only in good times and bad times. In order to stay perpetually happy, we should make an effort to be alive in each and every moment and enjoy it. This will always help us to stay happy and live a good life.

REMINDERS

- You are beautiful even on your worst days. Even when you don't feel like it, you are strong, unique, sensational and kind so don't let anything else make you feel otherwise.

- You were born to shine and rule this world with your smile. Stay focused no matter how doomed you think you are; you have a wonderful journey ahead.

- You are strong enough for every pain and every situation you face. Your strength is infinite and a moment of weakness cannot define it.

- The only person who is truly meant to love yourself is you because at the end of the day you are all you got.

- There is no better time to work on yourself than now because it is never too late to do something right for yourself.

- Everything you work on now will define what you are tomorrow, so keep working hard and make your future self, proud.

- Being happy is your own responsibility. You cannot burden someone else to do it for you.

- Happiness is nothing more than a positive mindset and perspective in life. Regardless of what the situation is, choose to be happy.

- Meditation will bring you closer to yourself and your peace of mind. Do it every day for at least 10 minutes, it will bring a lot of positivity in your life and get you closer to your spiritual self.

- The more you will accept yourself, the more you will love yourself and the more you will love yourself, the happier you will be. Remember it all starts with you.

- No matter what happens to you, stay grateful and always remember whatever happens is always for the best.

- Life will not always make it easy to be happy. It will keep throwing things and situations which will pull you down, but always remember this mantra even in your hardest times "All you have to do is find your way to happiness and everything else will be okay".

- What you think and focus on is what you will get in life. Hence, focus on loving yourself and staying happy and life will automatically present situations which will make you happy.

- Your life is a consequence of your beliefs because that is what becomes your reality. That is why always think good, see good and believe in the goodness around you and good things will follow.

- Happiness and sadness are two sides of a coin. You can flip this coin anytime you want. Hence, it is totally up to you which side of the coin you are looking at.

- In life everything does not work out the way you want it to be. If something does not work out, it is only because you deserve better. Learn to accept, let go and move on.

- Happy people don't do things differently, they just think differently. They see life from a positive side and find goodness even in the worst things around them.

- No problem or pain stays forever. Hence, no matter how difficult it seems at the moment, hold on, life has more in store for you and a new chapter will unfold.

- Your life will turn out the way you want it to be, just stay patient and don't stop believing.

- You can either keep crying and make your whole life miserable or you can smile and be happy and make your whole life beautiful. The choice is yours.

You have one life, live it to the fullest. No moment once gone comes back, hence live your each moment like it's your last.

CONCLUSION

Being happy is a choice we must make in each minute of each day regardless of what we are facing or going through in life. Through this book, I hope I could positively make your life better; help you find your way to happiness and push you towards living a lifetime of happiness. Happiness can be found in all the ways I mentioned above and by showering a little bit of kindness to the people around you. This can be done by complimenting others, smiling at strangers, leaving positive notes for people around you, buying food for the needy and so on. It does not take a lot to be happy and make others happy, all it takes is a small effort. One good effort, one good habit, one positive thought, one positive lifestyle will lead us to live a lifetime of positivity and happiness. It may not be easy following everything everyday but with consistent efforts we can reach where we always wished to be. Just do everything one day at a time. If we cannot change in a day, neither can our thinking and nor can our life. Life is a journey where we keep learning and growing at each stage and with everything we go through. Together, we can make this journey beautiful, fill it with love, joy and happiness. After all, it does not take a lot to be happy, all it takes is a genuine smile. So keep living, loving, smiling and spreading happiness everywhere you go.

POEMS

NEW SUNSHINE

1) Lost among old and gray
   Lies my shield of ray
   It is long gone they all say
   But I cried and wept and prayed

2) Tired and frustrated was my state
   Lost every hope and every gate
   All I could do was stand and wait
   And as I stood there I could not believe that was my state

3) Happiness, rainbow were long gone
   From whom one day I was born
   Like a piece of cloth which was torn and gone
   Which was one day forgotten by the world and never worn

4) I cried and beavered, shook and shivered
   Like an endless stream and an empty river
   I lost all my strength fell ill with fever
   Still something in my head told me I would one day fly high like a beaver

5) I was still not over, still not gone
I would one day show to the world I am not something sad and mourn
I could still stand up, fight and try
Even though all my efforts till now had been useless and dry

6) You can do it said the voice in my head
My mother's words my mind said
Now she was long gone and dead
But she was always with me; whenever
I was confused she was the one who led

7) Inspiration coloured me and a new motivation led
I knew I could do this was all my mind said
I thought of ways of doing this in my bed
In my life a new hope and happiness fed

8) You cannot actually win until you lose someone said
Now I know what they meant, you need to fall and get dents
Because until you cannot set up a strong tent
It is when you lose everything and your heart gets bent
You realise the meaning of love, peace and beautiful scent

9) And now as I recall that day I smile
Because it was a long time back and now it has been a while
All the problems we pile are nothing but after a while just a small tile

10) So my friends don't give up so fast
All your problems no matter how big they are won't last
After a while they will be your past
But what matters is how you face them, how much strength you got and how far you last
Because after this you will be a new and stronger person just like a different movie with a new cast
Hold on, hold on, hold on is all I will say
Because the people who stay strong and fight are the world's ray
They show a new beginning and a new way
But at the end of the day they are the ones who don't cry over a bad day or are stuck over stupid hay

11) You decide what you want to be, you decide what you want to do
But just make sure whatever you do you won't regret later
You would set your own traps and be your own better
And not turn something the world will hate later
Because if you don't take risks all you would turn out to be is a stupid waiter
So stand up and be a game setter
And watch the egg you planted hatch later

12) Because effort is all it takes to win this game
And write upon history your name
Take glory, pride and fame
And leave behind the reasons which were so lame
Because at the end of the day it will all be the same
To take glory, pride and fame

Dear reader,

Life is like a heartbeat with its continuous ups and downs. Nothing stays constant - not even pain or our failures. Hence, never give up and never stop trying in life no matter how many times you fall. Don't let your failures define you, your strength is way more than that. Each failure brings with it a learning which stays for life. Hence my dear readers keep learning, keep growing and keep smiling. Always believe in yourself and your dreams and always strive to be the best at everything you do. Don't let one bad chapter define the rest of your story. You were born to create magic, so don't stop until the whole world is filled with it. Lots and lots of love, warmth and happiness to you and to everybody around you.

CHILDHOOD MEMORIES

1) I wish I was a fairy the girl said,
Her dreams flew like wings as she lay in her bed
The story she had just heard was the reason of the thoughts which led
She was too small and didn't realise then that she would one day be the queen of the guy she would wed

2) Her thoughts circled and circled, her imagination grew
She thought of airship and those fearless crew
She wanted to be like them when she grew
Never realising that all these were just stories which were never true

3) She thought of Barbies and her dolls
And how she played cricket with her bat and ball
She thought of the promise her mother made to go to the shopping mall
And was happy that now she would buy her Barbie a prince which was handsome and tall

4) She had her own Barbie doll and kitchen set
And knew now her Barbie would have a prince and a perfect mate
They would look perfect together she would bet
And didn't know then that as she grew these were the things she would hate

These were the things which gave entry to adolescence and opened a new gate

5) She was perfectly happy with her thoughts as she lay
And was now waiting for a new beginning and a new day
Kids are innocent the world says
But they don't just build castles in the air
They dream out of reality and have a new version of the moon and sun's ray

6) Her mother smiled as she saw her sleep
And remembered her childhood at a flip
Those were the days she thought which were filled with happiness and pranks and can never be bought
Those cute and innocent eyes which looked at her after her mischief was caught
And how she smiled and never repeated the same mistakes after she was taught

7) She knew she would grow up and be a nice girl
With a pretty face and beautiful curls
And those little hands would soon be filled with responsibilities and heavy pearls
And she had to stop the tears which came at a hurl

8) Separation was too hard to take
She wanted to fill happiness forever in those little eyes with the cake she baked
And she knew that she soon had to walk alone and had to pass all the problems in the big lake

Make mistakes of all sorts and learn from them as she would wake
But she promised her little girl she would be in this journey with her for her sake

9) There are two different worlds in which they lived
One of a child filled with responsibilities and one of an adult with the responsibilities with which she was built
Her life full of work and duties with which she was filled
And now she looked at the young girl which time had killed

10) May god bless you was all her mind said
And wished she was showered with happiness and blessings which her mind fed
She would always be there for her when she needed any aid
And wished she would grow up to be strong and intelligent and was always the one who led

11) It is funny how time passes by she felt
Those cute dresses she wore once were now replaced with heavy belts
As she thought of her childhood her heart melt
And knew that one day her little girl would stand here and feel the same way for her daughter as time went

12) Where do we lose ourselves she thought
In school, college or in hope to reach another path
Where was the innocence lost

In school, college or in hope to reach another path
She knew now that whenever it was, it was always at a huge cost

Dear reader,

We all grow up too soon, never realising how time passes by. However, never let the child within you die. Learn to stay happy and carefree always. Grow as a person each day, each month and each year of your existence. Never let time or your age or the society stop you from doing anything. Always follow your heart even if it makes you do the craziest of things. Keep experimenting, keep living and love always. Every moment only comes once in your life so make the most of it and live it to the fullest. This is your life and your journey, so make sure it is beautiful. Lots and lots of love, warmth and happiness to you and to everybody around you.

PROUD EYES

1) She stood there so proud
As her child had risen up among the crowd
Her happiness was so high it had no ground
And now all she could hear for her girl was applause and sound

2) Her tears flowed, her eyes soft
She didn't know what to say yet her eyes said it all
She had seen her fight, she had seen her fall
And was happy that even after all that her child stood there so high and tall

3) She had crossed all problems, she had crossed all the walls
Her strength and determination had removed the pall
She didn't want to accept something low and float around like a ball
Nor did she want to be tossed around and not respected like a doll

4) She chose her own road, she chose her own way
And worked hard with each passing hour and each passing day
All she could see ahead was the future which way
And the bright sunshine and the sun's ray

5) She didn't give up when she fell
Even when she was tired with failures and her life felt like hell
These were the things which taught her a lesson and were a ringing bell
What made her keep trying no one could tell
But there was one thing for sure, she had made her mind to one day reach high and come out of that well

6) Don't ever give up my love you were never meant to lose her mother had said
When she was small she had told her about fairies and princess but had always given her a valuable lesson before going to bed
Her mother had always taught her beautiful and meaningful things and they all circled in her head
She wanted to do this for her mother, fulfil her dreams and shine out before she was dead

7) Now as she stood in front of her mother she could see how happy she was
It was like she wanted to capture that moment and stand there forever with a pause
But time didn't wait for anyone and soon she would be at a loss
Regardless she was happy now that she was the head and the new boss

8) Her mother shivered as she hugged her tight
She was old and wan and had lost her sight
She was happy that even when she had counted nights, her daughter would live forever and shine bright

9) Her words were not enough to tell her daughter how much she loved her
She tried to speak but her emotions blurred her
She just held her hand tight and kept it close to her heart
She wanted to live some more with her daughter and never part
But life had a different twist, a different game and its own way of throwing a dart

10) Her mother was breathing her last moments
I am very proud of you was her last comment
All you could see was pain in her eyes and her torment
And then she closed her eyes as if she was going through a dormant

11) She suddenly became motionless and her hand became bent
The daughter knew what that meant
She cried and cried until her eyes were red with paint
She shouted and yelled and wished for her mother to come back

As life had thrown her off guard and now she lay emotionless with her promotion letter and her new backpack

12) Now it all felt meaningless, the new promotion, the new office and being the new boss
It is true that in life everything comes at a cost
And even though she had been working for years to get that post, she now felt lost
It was like life had played its own game with her, picked her up and now she felt tossed

13) She remained lost for weeks but she was happy that at least she had completed her mother's dream before she was dead
She still missed her mother and had endless nights in her bed
But when anyone asked her 'I am fine' was all she said
And knew that her mother was always with her and even though she was dead when problems arise she was the one who led

14) Her mother soon became her inspiration and gave her a new light
Now it was like she wanted to do everything for her mother and fly high like a kite
She was no longer scared of dark and dreary nights
Because she knew that as long as her mother was with her she could reach any height

All she had to do was stay focused and never lose her end in sight

15) She missed her mother, she loved her every bit
But she had become her strength and was now part of her motivation kit
She wanted to take her mother's name high and wanted it to stay forever lit
After all it was her mother who had helped her when she was stuck in a pit

16) Her mother would stay forever in her heart and every bit
And all her teachings and values stayed with her and became her wit
Because after all she missed her mother and loved her every bit
But now she had become her strength and was now part of her motivation kit

Dear reader,
We all run so fast towards our goals that sometimes we fail to notice what stays back or what we are missing out on. Family is the most important thing. It is the only thing that stays when the rest of the world fades away. So give them time while you can, talk to them until you can and care for them as long as you can. We need to learn to balance our life and give time to everything that is important to us in order to avoid regrets. Being ambitious and running behind our goals is fine but it is important to stop for a second and realize at what cost are we doing that. Dear reader, wishing you a lifetime of abundant happiness, prosperity and success. Lots and lots of love, warmth and happiness to you and to everybody around you.

www.ingramcontent.com/pod-product-compliance
Ingram Content Group UK Ltd.
Pitfield, Milton Keynes, MK11 3LW, UK
UKHW040008200726
13854UKWH00001B/100